T0312182

Leadership as Meaning-Making

Leadership as Meaning-Making

Take the Hero's Journey to Transformation

John Varney

Routledge
Taylor & Francis Group

A PRODUCTIVITY PRESS BOOK

First published 2021

by Routledge
600 Broken Sound Parkway #300, Boca Raton FL, 33487

and by Routledge
2 Park Square, Milton Park, Abingdon, Oxon, OX14 4RN

Routledge is an imprint of the Taylor & Francis Group, an informa business

Library of Congress Cataloging-in-Publication Data

A catalog record for this title has been requested

ISBN: 9780367678265 (hbk)
ISBN: 9780367566043 (pbk)
ISBN: 9781003133001 (ebk)

Typeset in Minion Pro
by KnowledgeWorks Global Ltd.

Contents

Foreword

We live in times when meaning is slipping through the cracks and life is dominated (and threatened) by the conflict between powerful economic drivers on the one hand and, on the other, global crises that threaten the beauty of life on earth in all its diversity. As I write, the COVID-19 pandemic holds us all to ransom while it mocks the vulnerability of our so-called civilization. It is in this context that meaning-making leadership might just help save the day.

Leadership as meaning-making, John Varney reminds us, is an alternative to 'leadership as a lever of power,' as described in the 1994 paper of that title by Wilfred Drath and Charles Palus. The quarter-century since then has seen the popular concept of leadership increasingly conflated with power and control, at the expense of the idea of leadership as that flow of living energy between us that we equate with freedom and collective achievement.

My own contribution to leadership was in developing an understanding of the subtleties of teamwork and surfacing the hidden qualities that, as individuals, we bring to collective endeavour. The Belbin Team Inventory roles test is widely adopted, wherever people strive to transform collaborative groups into high-performing teams. These are the differences that make a difference! Varney builds upon these fundamentals in his development of the principles of the hero's journey – not as a path to fame and fortune, as some may imagine to be the hero's destination, rather I see Varney's hero more as a pioneer in the search for completion, wholeness, and maturity for the demanding role ahead.

In my lifetime, I have seen incredible changes in society and particularly in technology. Mankind is now incredibly powerful. However, I wonder whether there is enough wisdom to use that power to sustain human life as a fitting contributor to our living world. Perhaps, as Varney suggests in this book, the pursuit of personal transformation can, at this eleventh hour, save humanity from self-annihilation?

> —**Dr Meredith Belbin** is a researcher and management consultant, best known for his work on management teams. He is a visiting professor and Honorary Fellow of Henley Management College in Oxfordshire. His book *'Management Teams,'* released in 1981, pioneered the idea of team roles known as the Belbin Team Inventory.

Preface

WHO IS THIS BOOK FOR?

Maybe you are an entrepreneur or a manager or perhaps a teacher, cook, midwife, musician, plumber or parent. It matters not what you do for a living. What counts is whether you are looking for more significance. Perhaps the COVID-19 pandemic has given you pause for thought and you suspect that the old order was not as good as it claimed to be? Maybe your life has progressed along conventional lines yet, while appearing successful, leaves you with a touch of dissatisfaction? Whatever your role, you feel there must be more to life than the predictable journey towards retirement and old age. In this book, the leadership we are interested in, is your leadership. Living your own hero's journey is the way you, uniquely, will bring value to the lives of others, through making life meaningful.

The COVID-19 pandemic has paused some of our manic preoccupation with money and activity, allowing a little time for us to reflect on the values by which we live and whether we are in touch with our sense of purpose. It is with such a mindset that we may find ourselves wondering what we are doing and why. This book presents a practical philosophy for making a meaningful life and will, hopefully, provide insights to help you influence those with whom you work or otherwise relate.

The book is not 'the truth' – what, after all, is truth? But it provides a useful perspective on profound matters that affect us all. You may find these ideas expressed in different ways by wiser people than me, in which case, embrace them. Be prepared to find wisdom in many guises.

The book provides a framework for reflection. It alludes to the hero's journey – an archetype for our individual search for meaning and significance. The journey is typically described in mythical terms, as an adventure into the unknown from which the hero returns home, wiser and more mature, able to act as an elder in their community. In this context, being a hero has nothing to do with fame or glamour. This is a great cycle of being and becoming, a story told throughout history, in traditions around the world: a process available to every human.

The unknown worlds are already there within us, awaiting our awakening and discovery. The trials of the way may sometimes be in acts of daring-do but are just as likely to be in acts of care, compassion and quiet courage. These we have seen, for instance, in the responses of many key workers in relation to needs created by the COVID-19 pandemic. People have risen to the challenges, both within their metier and without, often risking their own lives for the greater good.

Such behaviour is reminiscent of the aftermath of World War II when, having shared fear and loss with strangers in other lands, people resolved not to return to the dysfunctions of the immediate pre-war period.

So, perhaps, we too have an opportunity to build a better and more wholesome society. But that must start with each of us, individually, awakening our awareness and developing our capability by venturing into the unknown. As you become more of what you can be, then you influence others and begin to practise your leadership as meaning-making. This, if we so choose, is how we might, together, bring into being a more wholesome society.

About the Author

 **John Varney** is founder-owner of High Trenhouse Centre for Management Creativity, based in North Yorkshire, UK. Formerly an architect, mountaineer and psychological group leader, John has helped organisations, from major internationals to community groups, to evolve strategies and manage change. On the way, he has helped many individuals to take charge of their lives.

I keep six honest serving-men
(They taught me all I knew);
Their names are What and Why and When
And How and Where and Who.

Rudyard Kipling

One to one coaching and on-line or face to face courses are available from www.centreformanagementcreativity.com

On-line materials are available for LogoVisual Thinking, as well as other developmental resources mentioned in this book.

john@high-trenhouse.co.uk

Introduction: Life-Cycles and the Hero's Journey

THE WAY WE ORGANISE OURSELVES IS MOSTLY MECHANISTIC

Our organisations are constructed on the lines of industrial era machines, a bit like clockwork mechanisms. We speak of chains of command, of leverage and gearing, of inputs and outputs, productivity, efficiency and so on. With such metaphors, people can come to be seen as no more than units of production – like the robots which will ultimately replace them. This way of treating life in mechanistic ways is pervasive. It spills into society and taints individual lives. Of course, our organisations could, if we so choose, be so much more than machine-like.

Meaningful living is a matter of our own personal choices and commitment but, when we allow ourselves to become parts of a machine (mere things) we lose independence of purpose. Without a sense of purpose, we are liable to be swept along by the whims of the day: what is 'in'; what is desirable, according to the media and to fashion. As we grow older, we may sometimes wonder why our living is lacking in meaning, until loneliness overwhelms us. But that is a result of choices we ourselves made at long forgotten points in our lives – choices to go with the whim and not with the substance; the choice to take instant pleasure, rather than investing for longer-term fulfilment – like livestock, happily fattening ourselves for slaughter. All this deprives us of resilience. As has been revealed to many by the lockdown of the global COVID-19 pandemic, the illusion of predictable control, promoted by the prevailing western scientific/economic paradigm (that reduces everything to quantities) has been shattered.

Resilience

A classic example of resilience is the reed that bends in the flood. Its capacity to yield to the force preserves it from being broken and, when the waters drop, it has the resources to recover its previous stance. The principle can be applied to any living system – not just plants but a person, a team, an organisation or community. Instead of resisting superior force to the point of breaking, one can develop the agility to yield and then to rapidly recover. Resilience, in the case of a person, is a complex relationship between physical, emotional and cognitive capacities that can be developed through training, experience and challenge. Similarly, for a larger social entity – a team, a company or community – resilience is a matter of relationships between component parts, with a degree of redundancy and flux. Such relationships reflect the maturity of the participants. But what is the nature of such maturity and how do we get it?

Consumer Society

In our modern global consumer society, propelled by supposed economic necessity, we are all under pressure to buy more stuff, to throw more away, to be less satisfied with what we have, to pay less attention. We work ever harder at unsatisfying work in order to earn money we can spend on consumption. None of this has been brought about for our benefit but to generate profits for people we will never meet. They, and we, are victims of the capitalist economic system. We go along with this narrative because it is the story of our time – the way things are. To think otherwise would require conscious struggle and intentional sacrifice. We would risk appearing diminished in the eyes of our friends – less hip, more primitive, less endowed – less ennobled in the prevailing superficial celebrity culture.

Thus, as revealed by the COVID-19 pandemic, society itself has been generally weakened and fragmented. Our ties to other people are often transactional and transient – we haven't the time, resources or inclination to develop any depth of contact – our closest relationships and even our self-perceptions are entangled in material goods and gadgets.

Society is fragmented because we have become fragmented, often allowing ourselves to be reduced to mere extensions of electronic devices.

Is There an Antidote?

We can gain much by collaboration – anti-fragmentarianism! – working with others to gain from synergies and shared resources but most of all, by raising one-another's thinking to a higher level, so that, together, we become more intelligent than any one of us apart. Co-thinking, co-creating and systemic self-organising are the means of countering fragmentation, recognising that everything is connected in some way to everything else and behaving accordingly, respecting the other and valuing their otherness.

There is a flow of energy and resources which follows our sense of purpose and, in so doing, gives meaning to our actions. I suggest that this flow is what we experience as leadership. Further, that leadership is not an exclusive property of important persons (so-called leaders) but is something to which we all contribute in our separate ways. As we become more aware of this phenomenon, we might build a better world.

Each of us has to find our own way to such meaning-making, maturity and wholeness. It may well not be what we believe is expected of us or what we have expected of ourselves. Each of us breaks new ground – every journey through life is unique. Nevertheless, a life cycle is so called because there is a universal cyclic pattern in the search for significance. This search, which brings us towards maturity and wholeness, is often referred to as the hero's journey.

The Hero's Journey

The Hero's Journey is an archetypal story form, well known to us, even from our childhood days. We come across it in the guise of ancient myths or fairy tales, of fantasy adventure stories or block-buster films. It has been around since the earliest oral storytellers brought history, myth and tradition to life for their audiences. Its cyclic form mirrors the cycles of nature that govern all life on earth. It is there in our narratives which, we will discover, can give form to visions and be shapers of strategies for success.

Modern versions of this cyclic narrative form were articulated by Joseph Campbell in his 'Hero with a Thousand Faces' and in a different way by Mary Douglas in 'Thinking in Circles.' The archetype will appear in different guises at different points in this book. There are distinct stages in any journey to maturity, each with its characteristic features. (Although some interpretations have as many as seventeen stages, I prefer to keep it to nine.) The hero leaves the world of ordinary existence in a quest for something exceptional. They have adventures, overcome difficulties (metaphorical giants, ogres, sirens, battles, aliens and stormy seas) and are helped by some agency to meet their ultimate challenge, which strips them of all illusions. In so far as they rise to their challenge, they return home with new understanding and new powers – they become whole unto themselves. Their new-found wisdom and maturity enables their leadership to bring meaning to the lives of others.

Without going into detail, this is the bald pattern.

1. The hero is happily pursuing life in whatever community they happen to find themselves.
2. They respond to a call of some kind, that unsettles their hitherto happy state of affairs.
3. They quit their ordinary life to embark on an adventure, leaving what is familiar to cross the threshold into unknown worlds – from the familiar towards the mythical, alien or divine.
4. In unfamiliar territories they have extraordinary experiences, discovering new capabilities as they are repeatedly tried and tested by successive challenges.
5. Having been toughened up a bit and having had their eyes opened, they find themselves propelled into the 'melting pot' of inner turmoil.
6. They reach a point of crisis and, as they rise to this mega-challenge, their old self perishes.
7. They awaken to their deeper, inner self with all else stripped away. In effect, they are reborn.
8. They turn towards home with new understanding, re-entering the known world and seeing it with fresh eyes.
9. Through their struggles on the homeward journey, their new knowledge is integrated into their very being, and they become increasingly whole unto themselves.
10. Inwardly transformed, they arrive where they started and enrich it through their deeper awareness.

If you seek a meaningful life, this hero's journey is worthy of deep reflection and contemplation, because it certainly applies to you! Of course, the heroism we need is not about celebrity or fame – it is unsung heroism and the journey itself may be metaphorical – simply a life-journey.

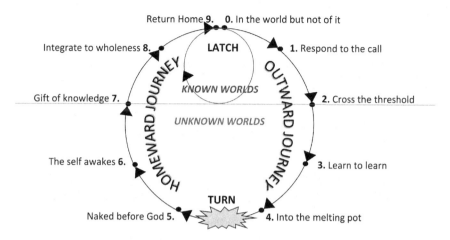

DIAGRAM 01.1
The hero's journey.

Wherever it might take you in the physical world, the real journey is one of inner exploration. Many people achieve inner transformation without ever leaving home and conversely, many people travel the world without ever maturing. In various chapters of this book we will explore aspects of the cyclic framework of inner development and how it applies to our own living and learning. We also explore how the pattern underlying the journey has similarities to the pattern behind many natural processes and phenomena.

Heroes and Leadership

Our title suggests that leadership is related to the hero's journey. Indeed, it is through leadership that people are helped on their journey of inner transformation and it is this process that makes work and life meaningful. Of course, we are not looking at leadership as usual – the stuff of popular training courses and many mainstream books. These tend to view leadership as what so-called leaders do within the controlling hierarchies of capitalist economics. They also often conflate leadership with management, power and hence, I am sorry to say, exploitation of many for the benefit of the few.

We shall return to the hero's journey later but meanwhile, in reading this book, you can discover your own deeper leadership. In the first chapter we meet the idea of different worlds of perception which, I suggest, describes the territory that the hero's journey explores – far beyond familiar everyday concerns and into little-known worlds that we all perceive but, most often, fail to recognise.

> 'We shall not cease from exploration – and the end of all our exploring will be to arrive where we first started and to know the place for the first time.'
>
> **–T. S. Eliot,** *Four Quartets*

EXERCISE 0.1: LEARN AS YOU GO!

At the end of each chapter there is a short exercise to help you clarify and assimilate the ideas. Allow yourself an hour for reflection. Have pen and paper to hand and make notes to yourself.

I recommend that you keep a journal during your reading of this book. Note your learning points and your insights, your experiences and especially any aspects on which you disagree with the text.

Right now, you could note the turning points of your own life and think about what stage you might be at, on your own life-journey to maturity and wholeness.

Feel free to email the author with your thoughts.

1

Worlds of Perception

An Adventure in Wholeness

WISDOM, MATURITY, AND WHOLENESS

More so than today, it used to be that older people were respected because they had a sense of perspective and a degree of wisdom. The maturing of a human being is a process of integration that brings them to wholeness. With life experience as their teacher, their heart learns to appreciate their head and their body to appreciate their spirit of adventure and enterprise. They learn to accommodate differences, to love, to be kind, to play their role, and to see patterns in the way events unfold. Their experience gives them a different perspective; wider, deeper, and more wholesome. Time brings them into harmony within themselves as living wholes, resonating with the life around them. This resonance is what we perceive as wisdom. Some people achieve such maturity even while they are young – others take longer. Some never get there. The process of maturing is a challenge for each of us.

The hero's journey (which can be anyone's journey to maturity) provides us with an archetypal metaphor for describing a person's life-voyage of discovery. However, we should be aware that it is a voyage, not to different lands, but through different worlds of perception. Although there may sometimes be an outer, physical journey, it is the inner journey that matters in relation to our maturation and integration as a whole person.

We are all capable of perceiving at many levels, from the concrete and tangible to the abstract and ineffable. Because we are embodied, we tend to focus on the physical perceptions of our senses and sometimes fail to take note of the more ephemeral perceptions that are gifted to us. We tend to see ourselves as physical beings trying to be spiritual rather than as spiritual beings coping with being incarnate.

To give ourselves a useful context for discussion, let us consider a framework comprising seven different kinds of perception:

1. Sensing,
2. Feeling,
3. Thinking,
4. Seeing,
5. Purposing,
6. Questing, and
7. Aspiring.

Most of us can recognise this differentiation of perceptions (regardless of what we might call them). We know we cannot touch a thought or move objects directly with our emotions. We all have hopes, experience flashes of insight and moments of bliss. If we are to be fully effective in the world, we need to develop new organs of perception to enable us to ratchet up and down, from the concrete to the abstract and back again. A physical problem requires a mental solution before we motivate ourselves into action to resolve it. We can live more completely (be more fully ourselves), if we open ourselves to more subtle levels of awareness.

As a young man, I used to hitchhike to the Isle of Skye and stay for as long as provisions allowed. A 3-day journey would get me to Glen Brittle where I would camp in a derelict cottage, in order to climb in the magnificent Cuillin mountains. Although the weather was often atrocious, I discovered that it was always worth the effort of going out 'onto the hill.' Nature was benevolent and would always reward me. I learned to value simple comforts and luxuriate in being alive. The physical aspect of such trips was rather ascetic, but, in overcoming inertia, I discovered life and beauty, almost as a separate reality, beyond the ordinary world of daily graft.

Perception has been likened to a mansion on many levels, of which the basement is where we spend most of our time. This is where we find ordinary existence, Sensing, Feeling, and Thinking – the world of daily discourse. However, we should not let ourselves be confined to the immediate tangibility of the basement because, above us, we might discover grand rooms with beautiful vistas. These higher levels, Seeing, Purposing, Questing, and Aspiring, have more freedom to maneuver and thus allow the creation of new possibilities. As heroes dare to venture into these domains, they learn to exercise more of their full potential.

I have worked one on one with many people, sometimes over periods of several years – long enough to witness extraordinary progress on their personal journeys. For example, I had a long association with an engineer in a national contracting company, from when he was first made a branch manager. Neither of us was sure what to expect from the other, but we co-created a fruitful and sustained relationship. Being by nature practical and down-to-earth, he was eager to think about his work in new ways so that he could innovate. Responding to his spirit of enquiry, I was privileged to help him address his challenges from an outside perspective. For two decades I worked behind the scenes on his presence and his thinking, providing support as he set up new parts of the enterprise and enhanced the effectiveness of older parts. Over the years our relationship evolved, as he progressed to regional manager, company director, then ex-director with special responsibilities and, eventually, to retirement. Always producing practical outcomes, we together explored different perspectives in order to innovate and to satisfy our spirit of enquiry. As well as working one to one, our collaboration extended to running team events, scenario building workshops, supplier collaborations, and industry research and development. Truly a hero's journey! In that period our relationship undoubtedly contributed significantly to the success of his organisation.

WORLDS OF PERCEPTION FRAMEWORK

Bearing in mind that not all perceptions are of the same substance, let us map out the territory we will traverse on the journey to maturity and wholeness. It is as if our perceptions are nested one within the other, from the most concrete to the most abstract. I do not claim this to be 'the truth' and nor is it scientific. However, most people instantly recognise it and I recommend you entertain it as a useful way of seeing things. All these perceptions will, of course, be familiar to you, although you may not be used to differentiating them in this way.

World 1: Sensing

From infancy, we learn about the physical world through the five senses of touch, sight, hearing, taste, and smell. Guided by parents and teachers, we construct images in our minds of what all those various inputs represent. As we learn to name the parts (Mama, sweety, bath time, etc.), we begin to construct our world! Much of our later life is devoted to reinforcing our early constructs. How we do things manifests in patterns of our behaviour. At the interface between this physical domain and our motivations, are ingrained patterns we call habits.

World 2: Feeling

Distinct from our senses, we experience flows of energy. Beyond mere 'fight or flight,' we harness this emotional or motivational energy to direct our physical capacity to get things done. Emotional energy is often socially connected, so that, along with colleagues and friends, we can be swept along with the flow. Our visions and ideas, from a more abstract level, help us to direct this energy, but it can easily be influenced by others. Ingrained patterns of thinking that direct energy down well-worn channels are called assumptions.

World 3: Thinking

Our cognitive capabilities build patterns of experience by which we 'make sense.' We name common patterns and learn structures of meaning. Through language, we understand the particular domain in which we are socially embedded. Patterns crystallise as knowledge – practical know-how, professional know-how, my history, my geographies, and my relationships. When we 'know' where we are and what is going on and grasp the principles of cause and effect, we are able to act and create, rather than merely reacting to external stimulus. On the other hand, fixity of patterns appears as attitudes that can blind us to what is.

These first three worlds comprise our ordinary existence. Now we are at a threshold, beyond which the hero (and we) can venture into lesser-known territory – territory that is not entirely unknown to us but is less well-known, because we often shrug off higher perceptions as if they were aberrations. As we pay attention to higher worlds, we begin to develop 'new organs of perception.' Through practice we can become more familiar with the realms of our metaphysical existence. Then we might return to our everyday world and see it with new eyes.

World 4: Seeing

Beyond that painstaking structuring of patterns, which we call thinking, we are also capable of 'Seeing.' Occasionally, we can instantly recognise the complex interconnections of a greater whole. When we 'see' we do so clearly, all at once. 'Seeing' is a meta-knowing, which grasps a totality and can therefore organise, as patterns of possibility become visible. Perception of a whole complex pattern also enables us to intuit missing parts or at least to see where we need to look more closely. The same faculty enables us to see unrealised futures, in which case we call it 'Vision.' This can be anything that we are able to imagine but which remains provisional until given substance by our intent. Our seeing is moderated by values (guides to what is acceptable, which can change and evolve).

World 5: Purposing

Where Seeing recognises a possibility, Purposing chooses a direction. Sharing a Sense of Purpose with others is unifying and therefore gives us a shared identity. Being purposeful is sufficiently broad in scale and in time, that it can encompass many linked visions. Purpose becomes a 'strange attractor' within the fractal patterns echoing throughout our system. Hence, having a Sense of Purpose creates order and gives life meaning. Without purpose, our acts are arbitrary. Meaning, Purpose and Identity are valuable to us individually and in our collective endeavours. A Sense of Purpose may require many visions to be realised and will provide a guiding framework for all steps that lead to action. Here, we come across the barrier of our beliefs, which can be powerful enablers but might also limit our capacity to embrace new possibilities.

World 6: Questing

Beyond such shared identity, we can quest further into intangible worlds. Using intuition, we can, with practice, tune into the winds of change, surveying fields of potential, recognising peaks and troughs of possibilities, seeking out areas of high potential or safe havens, so positioning ourselves to enjoy optimal circumstances as our future unfolds. Scanning fields of emergent relationships between patterns as they interact, we learn to identify potential changes as opportunities or threats. We can hone such strategic awareness to amplify weak signals of impending futures, helping us determine useful purposes and to make profound choices.

World 7: Aspiring

We ultimately live in a world of spirits – a world beyond dreams. In the story of Odysseus, this would be the domain of the Gods and it is maybe less unfamiliar than we generally admit. We are all familiar with the spirit of adventure, spirit of enterprise or spirit of solidarity, and many others. We can discover our free spirit and with it, the capacity to view dispassionately all the worlds described in the previous page. To aspire means 'to long for' and also 'to breathe.' The breath of life gives substance to the most abstract form of our existence.

WORLDS WITHIN WORLDS

As we become aware of such a hierarchy of perceptions, we learn how to navigate it – how to determine where we are at any moment and how to get to where we wish to be. Diagram 1.1 provides a kind of map - a schematic of how the worlds relate and words we commonly use to describe experiences without knowing how they fit. Using this map, we can learn to bring about changes; by inspiration and reflection, we can attune to the wider patterns of the cosmos, embracing natural spirituality, compassion, and love.

Because we have bodies, we continuously interact with the physical domain, where we see the results of our actions. However, we can be most effective in those concrete realms when we approach them from the more abstract. For instance, we are familiar with the concept of 'an idea whose time has come.' Even though such ideas have no physical form, they can powerfully influence physical affairs. The physical world is the most constrained and the more abstract worlds have increasing degrees of freedom.

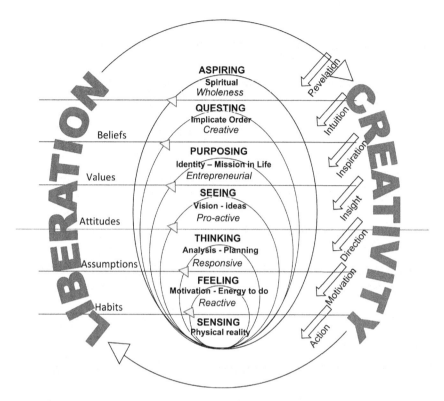

DIAGRAM 1.1
Worlds of perception

Physically we are obliged to deal with the here and now. However, our imagination can take wings. Especially, courage, hope, faith, and love are attributes of higher worlds of perception.

So, for example, someone may perhaps aspire to bring about a wholesome society and adopt a purpose of improving social cohesion. Within that they may see the possibility of forming a model community, to which end they might bring together diverse people with appropriate skills and engage with them in exploring possibilities. Eventually their vision will produce strategies and plans that result in action.

THE BREATH OF LIFE

Our perceptions can move up and down the scale, from the most concrete to the most abstract and back again. This cycle is the Breath of Life in which we all participate. Ideally, it enables all our actions to be inspired and thereby effective. From observation, we are drawn to create ideas and visions. Through inspiration we produce strategies and plans, tactics, and action. The ability to find freedom in navigating this hierarchy is a sign of the mature individual; one who is whole and enjoys inner freedom.

If we allow ourselves to be confined to the basement of our mansion, we may be physically present but not be well motivated and rarely think before we act. We may experience conflict between what we want to be doing and what we think we 'should' do. As we dither, we dissipate our energies. We may even spend most of our life this way, anaesthetising ourselves with food, drink, sex, and shopping, while never feeling fulfilled. This happens to many of us. To avoid such a fate we need to become more aware and more conscious, to explore our higher potential, and make our own meaning. We need to listen for our calling and embark on our own hero's journey through those higher realms and dare to explore the limits of our potential. Then, our leadership can be an inspiration to others.

FINDING INNER FREEDOM

First, habitual behaviours hold us in repeated patterns. Some habits are useful – others bog us down and cause harm. Habits take our energies down well-worn channels. In this sense, some habits can be barriers to progress. Breaking a habit, even a good one, releases energy and gives us greater freedom.

Second, every action is necessarily based on assumptions, but often we are subjected to assumptions that cripple our capabilities. This can be especially true when we assume how someone else will respond to our actions or what someone else is thinking. Self-talk, based on assumptions, can weaken our resolve and render us immobile. We need to break free from limiting assumptions.

At a more subtle level, our ability to embrace new possibilities can be severely constrained by limiting attitudes which determine what visions we might entertain. Such thoughts as 'it can't be done' or 'I am not really worthy' can shut down all initiative, whereas a can-do attitude will open doors.

At a more abstract level still, our identity and sense of purpose are governed by our values. Values are subtle rules of mind, rooted at that purposive level, that ultimately determine what is acceptable in the way we do things. Beyond values, our beliefs affect the fields of endeavour in which we choose to operate and what we seek to make of our life. As we move up the hierarchy of our perceptions, the barriers become more subtle yet are more powerful in their effect. Breaking those subtle patterns in our minds enables us to enjoy the freedom of our finer perceptions. Our hero's journey tests our limitations and challenges us to break new ground.

... AND USING IT TO GOOD EFFECT

Action comes about when our motivation moves us physically. Our cognitive capability gives that motivation direction. Seeing inspires our planning. Insight informs us where to focus. Intuition helps us grasp the pattern of things and revelation illuminates possibilities of what can be. Then the hero's return journey becomes a cascade, from our finest most abstract perceptions, into the world of our everyday actions.

One could say that, when we are fully present and fully alive, we span between these extremes of possibility – from the concrete to the ineffable. We can progress in our ability to perceive in every domain. We must act in the physical world, but the wellspring of our actions can be at any level. As we develop personal maturity, the power to move between worlds of perception becomes properly ours, giving us the ability to choose where that wellspring will arise. The process of maturing gives us the facility to move freely to whichever level we choose. The hero is restored firmly to the earth and their wholeness bestows the inner freedom to live equally in every world between earth and heaven, as depicted in the biblical imagery of Jacob's Ladder (Genesis 28:10–19).

Of course, this is not science! Science, technology, and daily life are mostly confined to the basement of our mansion! Nevertheless, it gives us a framework for thinking about the full range of our perceptions, which are part of our inner reality. This framework enables us to gain a deeper understanding of the nature and potential of our possible progress to maturity.

FINDING SIGNIFICANCE – THE HERO'S JOURNEY

The road to maturity requires that we take that hero's journey in some form or other, according to our predilections and the opportunities that present themselves. Leaving our ordinary existence in response to a call, we venture into different worlds of perception, learning as we go. If, as, and when we are transformed, we can return to the mundane world and see it with fresh eyes, in order to relieve its shallowness and lack of significance. Looking at life this way we can readily see that wealth and comfort, worldly success, and attachments are no more than distractions. They tend to cushion us from the drama of living our own unique life to the full, of becoming all that we can be and thus achieving an inner state of wholeness in place of mere outward show.

In this first chapter, we have introduced a framework that suggests a full life requires us to venture forth. We need to listen for the call to go beyond the comfortable world of our youth and everyday living, so that we can be exposed to transformational experiences. We can claim our right to inhabit every level. Indeed, the concept of levels can be useful in our quest for maturity, to give substance and credence to our leadership. In the next chapter, we will begin to explore the cyclic nature of our every action, especially in relation to breaking new ground. The hero's journey into metaphysical domains is a fractal, reflected at every scale of human endeavour.

EXERCISE 1: IDENTIFY DIFFERENT
WORLDS OF PERCEPTION

Does any of this ring true to you? (Make notes)

- Can you differentiate different worlds?
- Can you identify anything in your own experience that suggests that 'higher worlds' exist?
- Identify specific examples of your own experience of each world of perception.
- Think about how, in your experience, such worlds manifest in your everyday life.
- Think of examples of where you felt locked in the basement and how you found more freedom.
- How would it be if you were free to elevate the wellspring of your actions in particular situations?

Note specific examples.

2

The Creative Cycle

And the Enneagram Framework

CREATIVITY IS EVERYWHERE

Venturing into unknown worlds is a creative process. It is our creativity that enables us to address novel situations and deliver novel outcomes and yet it is also there in even the most mundane actions. We participate in countless cyclical creative processes daily – overlapping at every scale and every moment. This is mostly below the level of our consciousness, so, when we meet more complex challenges, we need to become more aware.

At the school of architecture we were taught about design, but it was not revealed to us that there was a structure to the process of creativity. I first studied the structure of processes at Bennett's International Academy at Sherborne House. There were a hundred students, resident for a year, eager to listen to talks, learn Gurdjieff movements, act, sing, meditate and do practical work. Learning was earthed in practice, which occupied most of the time. It largely took the form of renovation and maintenance of the former stately home itself, as well as restoring the gardens to productivity, housekeeping, and manning the kitchen. Each day a different person had the role of head cook, responsible for organising a mostly inexpert group of fellow-students to prepare food for the community. This gave us an excellent medium for the study of self and the structure of process.

Three times per day the kitchen waited to come to life in a new cycle, starting with breakfast, which was relatively straightforward. Then, as head cook, you needed to find out what was available from the garden or from the minimal stock (budgets were very tight and choice limited) and to devise appropriate dishes for lunch and dinner, within the competence of your crew. The kitchens were left over from a bygone era, so their operation was primitive – lots of handwork and challenges of managing available heat and eliminating waste, while producing sometimes tasty-meals from inadequate or unexpected ingredients. You allocated responsibilities to the largely unskilled team, according to perceived capability, to ensure that meals were decently served to your hungry customers. There was high drama as mealtimes approached and often much creativity was involved, in order that the customers should not know how close to disaster their food had been. The system certainly gave us great opportunities to examine collective creative processes.

THE CREATIVE CYCLE

An important feature of how novelty emerges through time is the movement from the concrete to the abstract and the return from the abstract to the concrete. For the new to emerge, the old has to give way. DIVERGENCE, alternating with CONVERGENCE, pulses through the process. As in the hero's journey, the midpoint – the change of direction – is characterised by uncertainty and usually experienced as tension or crisis. Bearing with uncertainty, divergence, and indecision, until the 'creative spark' occurs, brings about creativity and leads to innovation. However, where people feel a need to manifest decisiveness (typically managers under pressure), they may be tempted to prematurely release the tension, thus short-circuiting creativity and producing mediocre outcomes.

In our diagram, each point provides a particular input by which the temporal process increases its potency. The circle represents a progression in linear time as indicated by the arrows.

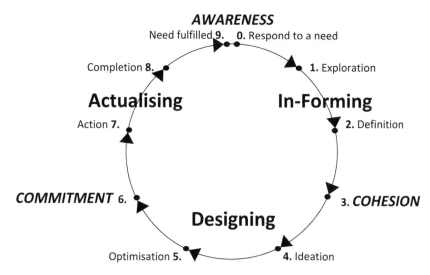

DIAGRAM 2.1
The creative cycle

I will describe the generic creative process (which applies to processes at every scale) from the perspective of the kitchen at Sherborne. I hope you will be able to follow it and I recommend you explore how the framework makes sense to you, personally, in whatever processes you commonly engage. See if you can identify details of this framework in specialist interests of your own.

A process kicks off when our awareness of need is strong enough to overcome indifference, inertia, and other priorities. **Awareness** is a critical factor, a function of attention rather than something to be done. It enables us to identify, out of all possible activity, what will be the focus of our particular process. Finding yourself, as head cook, responsible for feeding a hundred people, under-resourced and on a tight timescale, certainly helps focus attention! Now you need to share your contained anxiety with your scratch team of inexpert helpers.

This will enable you to move into **Exploration,** where you gather information relevant to the challenge. In the kitchen, you need to know what ingredients are available – in the refrigerator, in the store, what is ripe in the garden. What skills do you have at your disposal? Who can do what, and how will they best be deployed to turn those ingredients into something appetising? How can you best use the available culinary equipment to effect the transformation of ingredients into palatable food? What dietary requirements do your diners have and are there special guests? Without exploration, we might have no idea what information is needed or where to begin to look. Apart from what will go on in the kitchen, exploration includes knowing who you will be feeding, how the food will be presented to the diners, and how the dining room will be set up for the occasion.

All this is clearly divergent in nature. However, at some point, convergence will be needed for the process to move on. Convergent thinking focuses the enquiry into a **Definition** or specification of some kind. Its nature varies according to the circumstances but, in the kitchen, it takes the form of a vision of what the final effect will be for the diners and hence a menu of dishes, within the capability of those involved. This is more concrete than was possible at the focus stage, informed as it is as a result of all that exploration.

If we are to proceed, we need to hold together as a whole – without **Cohesion** we easily fall prey to procrastination, dispute about roles and process, or other dysfunction that dissipates our attention. Cohesion sustains relationships between the players, encouraging conversations or interactions by which ideas are scattered and shaken to converge in new constellations. Cohesion is a quality of being – the capacity to sustain productive relationships through thick and thin, through countless acts of leadership by all involved. Where a group is involved, such cohesion will be called teamwork. The chief cook will engender the players' confidence that, between them, they can manage the risky process of giving birth to a meal that will delight the community.

With cohesion, we now enter the design phase, the early part of which is characterised by **Generation** of diverse ideas for selecting, preparing, and cooking the ingredients. The chief cook will need conversations with each player and all, to ensure the challenge will be met. They will discuss recipes and processes, resources and experience, seeking the best possible outcome. Alternative possibilities are entertained and tested in the imagination. Even as the design is being finalised, new ideas keep popping up.

Eventually the creative flow has to be constrained, to enable the process to move towards realisation. The second part of the design phase, then, is convergent in nature, as it will need commitment of resources to complete the process. Our solution will be the best we can produce, from the ideas we have gathered, within the constraints we have. As chief cook, we will breathe life into it, a 'touch of magic' that enables us to see the outcome and will win the resources to bring it into reality. If all goes well, we will experience a dramatic integrative step, wherein the multiplicity of ideas gels into one whole concept of a successful meal – more than the sum of its parts.

This step is typified by **Optimisation** of the design, so that the players can commit to bring it into reality and to ready themselves for action. Cookbook illustrations, kitchen and dining room walk-throughs, mock-ups and rehearsals combine with calculations that anticipate everyone's buy-in to realising the feast.

So, we come to the point of **Commitment**. Until this point is reached, everything has been represented virtually – in imagination, on paper, or as prototypes. Now we are going to make it real. This is very different from all that has gone before and will be the ultimate test of our process. If commitment is not forthcoming, we will be obliged to repeat earlier stages, to compromise or abandon the project altogether. Commitment is not an action but a decision – an act of will. If there is not the will, the project is stillborn. As chief cook we will be persuasive but not manipulative, because without genuine commitment, there may be deviation, failures, and regrets.

When there is the will, the process will enter the field of **Action** with all the uncertainties and unexpectedness that entails. Whatever we thought in the earlier stages is now being made real – no longer 'just' a concept. Entry to the field of action invariably brings surprises; it is rarely just what we anticipated. As we cut the vegetables or probe the chickens, our ideas may need to flex. At this stage of the process, resources and energy begin to be expended – eggs are broken, heat is dissipated. Even as we act, things change around us. We, therefore, need to be divergent in our thinking so that we respond to the emerging reality, rather than adhering strictly to the book or the plan. This stage is dramatic in nature, as it deals with emergent phenomena such as substitution of ingredients or discovery of unexpected skills (or lack thereof).

Eventually, the nature of our work changes once more to convergence, as we begin homing-in on our goal in the process of **Completion**. We strive to close the gap between the state of play and the ideal finished product our diners expect – and when they expect it. This is a case of finishing dishes, timing everything to be hot and ready at the right moment, adding finishing touches, and, not least, getting everything ready to present at the table. It ends when the diners gasp with delight as they taste their first bite.

Finally, our diners are actually enjoying the meal we have prepared, savouring good food and delighting in the whole occasion. The kitchen enabled the ingredients to be transformed and also enabled the transformation of those inexperienced cooks. Now it is returned to a condition of readiness – dishes washed and put away, surfaces wiped, floors mopped, ready for the next cycle to begin. The cooks can review the results of their efforts and draw their own lessons – the fruit of shared endeavour. All experience the satisfaction of achievement and the benefit of lessons learned. The need is fulfilled.

TEAM ROLES

With this view of the processes by which things come about, we can reflect on the different roles that enable us to complete the cycle. At each stage, a particular kind of relationship work is required, in addition to technical contributions. Because of our predilections, we each bring differing strengths and weaknesses at different stages. Hence, we will usually be better off when we can harness the diverse talents of a group, lest some roles are left unfilled. Spontaneous groupings can often be more effective than many so-called teams, in which someone with authority determines who will do what and when.

Dr Meredith Belbin researched management 'team roles' and identified eight different roles people play. Later, with some hesitation, he added a ninth, 'the Specialist.' Belbin did not sequence the roles or offer any schematic of the process they supported. Although his names for the roles may seem a bit obscure, they become clearer when mapped on to the creative cycle. The cycle clarifies the nature of the different roles and their interdependence. Belbin's work (published in 1981) was based on psychometric tests in the context of a management team exercise. The generic creative cycle was developed by Centre for Management Creativity (based loosely on the enneagram and extensive studies conducted in the 70s by J. G. Bennett) and also subsequently tested with many management teams.

Point on Enneagram	Creative cycle attributes	Belbin's team roles
0	Awareness	Specialist
1	**Exploration**	Resource Investigator
2	**Definition**	Team Worker
3	Cohesion	Coordinator
4	**Ideation**	Plant
5	**Optimisation**	Monitor evaluator
6	Commitment	Implementor
7	**Action**	Shaper
8	**Completion**	Completer Finisher
9	Need fulfilled	Specialist

DIAGRAM 2.2
Attributes and roles of creative process

We will look more closely at team roles in Chapter 6, but meanwhile here are Belbin's roles mapped against the attributes of the creative cycle. Use Belbin's names if you are familiar with them, although personally, I find his names confuse the role with the person and therefore I prefer the more abstract attributes.

Specialists tend to top and tail the process, although specialism is not itself a team role. Furthermore, specialists are quite often not very good team players or simply do not see the need. It may well be, therefore, that they are best positioned as resources external to the team itself.

THE ENNEAGRAM

What I have called the Creative Cycle is a simple take on a subtle and powerful pattern of process called the enneagram (from the Greek, meaning a nine-sided figure). Though its source is enigmatic, the enneagram was

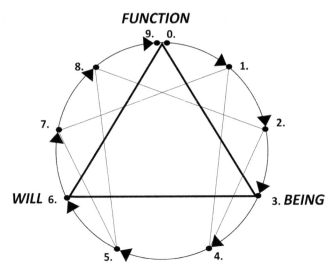

DIAGRAM 2.3
The Enneagram

taught by Gurdjieff to his followers in St Petersburg more than a 100 years ago before he brought it to the west in the 1920s. I learned about it from Bennett in the 60's.

There are two branches of enneagram studies, one of which is focused on structure of processes. The other, which is focused on personality types (Palmer and others) is not relevant to us here. The enneagram reveals a generic structure that can stimulate exploratory conversations about processes at any scale and for any discipline. We have looked at the outer circle which I call the creative cycle, and now we will consider the triad before we look briefly at the inner lines.

THE TRIAD: AWARENESS, COHESION, COMMITMENT

An important feature of the enneagram is the triad (triangle of interacting impulses) formed by points 9/0, 3 and 6. This is the core dynamic of interactions without which there would be no process. The triad is timeless and represents aspects of being and becoming that accumulate as a result of the temporal unfolding represented by the circle.

The process unfolds over time in three phases. Firstly, awareness of the issue engages us in seeing a solution: a reaching forward into an end state when the challenge has been met. Secondly, such awareness involves cohesion – Holding together multiple factors while being co-present with the issue to be resolved, and also evoking the solution in the present moment. We make the connection between the present and the future through a process of design and realisation. Thirdly, for anything to happen, we need commitment – an act of will.

We can see that the three corners of the triangle are parameters of our state of maturity (whether as individual, team, community or organisation). They are not 'in time' – that is, they exist and accumulate because of the temporal process they are sustaining. Has the individual (or the team) the functional awareness, the cohesive capacity and the entrepreneurial intent to meet the challenge? Between these three, in the flow of time, progress is achieved through the alternation of divergent thinking and convergent thinking.

THE INNER DYNAMICS

The inner lines suggest connections that are not in linear sequence but connect across that sequence to enable progress to be made. The lines follow the sequence 1, 4, 2, 8, 5, 7, which number (recurring) happens to be 1 divided by 7. The idea is that the simple linear sequence of the outer circle is complemented or supported by an inner flow. Every intermediate point is connected to two others, one that builds on a less complete stage and one that anticipates a more complete stage.

1, 4, 2, 8, 5, 7 recurring! The process is iterative and each iteration brings an enrichment of the outcome as well as enrichment of the people involved.

The conversations we need in order to discover more about the topic of interest, can be enriched by mapping our responses according to this unique framework. One part of the diagram, the outer circle relates to linear time, whereas the inner lines relate to flow of information and energy. Each point has two inner connections that influence it, one fed by *past* experience and one anticipating a *future* state of affairs. The triad is timeless and is enriched and strengthened by each cycle of the process. This enrichment is the maturing or integration of whatever entity is involved, epitomised in the hero's journey.

Fuller studies of the enneagram framework will be found in J. G. Bennett's *Enneagram Studies*, Anthony Blake's *The Intelligent Enneagram*,

Point 1 — Our exploration is informed by reference to the action phase, point 7, and also to ideation, point 4—our search for relevant information is not a blank sheet because we know roughly where to look and what we seek.

Point 4 — Idea generation is clearly shaped by the interaction of information gathered, point 1 and the specified objective, point 2.

Point 2 — We are able to specify because we anticipate that we can solve the problem, point 4 and also complete the process, point 8.

Point 8 — Completion is a realisation of the outcome specified at point 2, refined by the optimal solution identified at point 5.

Point 5 — That design solution anticipated the action at point 7 would achieve the completion at point 8.

Point 7 — Action is fed (and constrained) by the exploration at point 1 and the design of point 5, which points to completion at point 8.

DIAGRAM 2.4
The inner dynamics

Saul Kuchinski's *Systematics* and with well-illustrated examples, in Richard Knowles's *The Leadership Dance*.

We will expand on the diversity of roles in relation to co-creation in Chapter 6. In this chapter, we have looked at the generic structure of creative processes – something that is reflected in our hero's journey to maturity and that our own leadership can employ in the making of meaning. In the next chapter, we will further explore the triad and some of the ways we act in the world, by which we learn to learn. By learning at different levels, we become more of what we can be. In so doing, we practice leadership of self and others.

EXERCISE 2: GET A FEEL FOR THE PROCESS ENNEAGRAM

Have a piece of paper or a whiteboard handy

Think about how your principal activity (what you do for a living or what you are passionate about) plots on to the creative cycle. Can you identify the three main divisions and the convergent/divergent aspects of each? Plot it all on your own diagram. The start point is where you are now with no more than an idea. The full circle gets you to where the idea has been made a reality.

- Can you identify the different stages of your process?
- What does the main triangle mean in your experience?
- Can you identify the inner sequence of influences?
- Does any of it ring true for you?
- Think about other activities in which you engage – how well can you plot any of them on to the creative cycle?

3

Being and Becoming

The Triad of Inner Development

OUR THREEFOLD BEING

The triad of awareness, cohesion, and commitment, identified in the last chapter, shows up as a familiar pattern in our behaviours – the way we act in the world. Three richly interrelated questions we might ask ourselves before we act are; **What?, How?, and Why?**

The triad is in the DNA of even the simplest action, for example: **'What?'** – *I will make a cup of tea.* **'How?'** *Using the best china or just a teabag in a mug? Will I pour milk from the carton or put it into a jug first? Will I serve tea on a tray or not bother?* And **'Why?'** (which will invariably affect the How and What) – *Tea for a visitor? Tea for the decorator? Tea to impress a client?* Each possible **'Why?'** will have a different response. So, the three terms of the triad interact in the whole process – even of making tea! How much more complex will be their interaction regarding my son's university education, my choice of a new home, or planning to double the size of my business? But throughout the full span of my actions, the same basic triad is present.

SKILL, CAPACITY, AND INTENT – SCI

Looking at any individual, those three aspects manifest as;

1. Technical skill and knowledge (determine **What** the individual can do),
2. Their capacity (determines **How** confidently they tackle the task and how well they handle setbacks, uncertainty, and complexity), and
3. Their intent (determines **Why** they might choose a particular action).

We are fairly good at developing skill and knowledge – it is relatively easy, because it can be communicated, measured, and tested. Much of our education is of this ilk.

Developing confidence, trust, and the capacity to bear with uncertainty or complexity, to deal with setbacks or cope with crises, is more subtle. It is a function of emotional intelligence and inner fortitude. It grows over time as we learn from experience. Provided we are able to learn from it, many of us grow our capacity in the school of hard knocks, with all its successes and also, especially, its failures.

Developing intent – our will (not to be confused with willpower or self-will) is often left to chance. Intent grows as we exercise it. We do this by taking on challenges of all kinds, gradually upping the ante to ensure that whatever we are doing is stretching us a little.

In the early days of our experiment at High Trenhouse, we had a rather naïve aim to become self-sufficient. To this end we opted for low income and low expenditure, which necessitated doing everything ourselves, living close to the land and eating frugally. Struggling to cope in very basic conditions – no drains and no heating – we boldly bought a cow and then had to find out how to get milk out of her. Her name was Suzie, a beautiful Jersey, who became my teacher! She taught me patience, tolerance, and humour. I was not her only student, as all our visitors took a turn at milking her.

Cows produce a great deal of milk – relentlessly! They do not respond to a sign saying 'no milk today.' We certainly could not drink it all and, because we could not afford waste, had to discover how else to make use of it. As the time went by, we learned to make yoghurt and, by straining the surplus we made quark, which became an ingredient in a wonderful cheesecake we could freeze. With the cream, we made pure dairy ice-cream

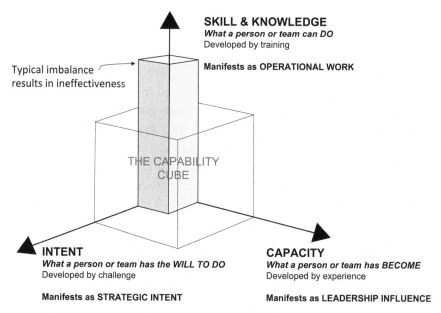

SKILL & KNOWLEDGE
What a person or team can DO
Developed by training

Typical imbalance
results in ineffectiveness

Manifests as OPERATIONAL WORK

THE CAPABILITY
CUBE

INTENT
What a person or team has the WILL TO DO
Developed by challenge

Manifests as STRATEGIC INTENT

CAPACITY
What a person or team has BECOME
Developed by experience

Manifests as LEADERSHIP INFLUENCE

DIAGRAM 3.1
Skill, capacity, and intent

and we also developed an excellent soft cheese with a good shelf-life, feeding the whey to the pigs. Bull calves were reared for meat. What we could not consume, we sold. What did not sell, we consumed. This wonderful little enterprise enabled us to keep more cows and the products were so good, we still had folk calling 10 years after the last cow had departed.

This illustrates the threefold nature of development; the growing **capacity** for enterprise, the **intent** to make it sustainable, and the increasing **skill and knowledge** of good husbandry.

In our society, we tend to focus on 'skill and knowledge' (what can be measured) at the expense of other parameters. Balancing the three maximises the capability of each person and each relationship, at the scale of individuals, teams, or whole organisations. If any of the three is weak, effectiveness is compromised. To grow these aspects of capability in balance, to live fully, and learn to work effectively, is a worthy lifelong aim for every human. Skill and knowledge, capacity, and intent grow symbiotically as interdependent dimensions of learning. Look at the diagram 3.1 and you will get the idea that our capability equates to the volume enclosed by all three dimensions which, when balanced, comprise a cube of capability. The process of maturing – integration as a living whole – has the effect of increasing the size of the cube.

Of course, these characteristics are not confined to individuals or their organisations. They apply in every human domain and to social structures at every scale. When I joined a small architectural practice in Richmond, I had an artist, Paul Riley, as workmate. We quickly struck up a close and dynamic relationship through which he learned from me the finer points of architectural detailing and I learned from him to look beyond the bounds of convention. The fact that he never subscribed to the idea that something could not be done, gave him an extraordinary creative drive. He was not afraid of making mistakes and, with inexhaustible or elastic capacity, his intent could be directed as he chose. As a result, overcoming any deficit of skill or knowledge was only ever a matter of time. His gifts were an asset to any group faced with a challenge in any domain.

We applied these same principles to our occasional trips to the mountains, where I was in my element and he, although outside his comfort zone, was ever curious. I well recall one occasion, after a demanding week in the office, we drove 5 or 6 hours and hiked a couple more before pitching our tent in the wild. Next morning, we set out to complete several rock-climbing routes, finishing on the summit of the highest peak in England. Returning late to our camp, we were too exhausted to consume anything other than endless brews of sweet lemon tea. An easier day followed before the return journey to London. The whole experience was demanding, challenging, exciting, and exhausting. Its success had required bold strategy, a dynamic relationship between us, skill, exertion, and abundant good humour. The outcome was profound mutual enrichment, which gave meaning to all our exertion. How grateful I was to have enjoyed such wonderful companionship on such a beautiful and rewarding adventure.

After many excursions of that ilk, I began to realise that I did not mountaineer just for personal pleasure, but for the opportunities such activity gave me to open the eyes of others to their own deeper perceptions.

DEVELOPING CAPABILITY

Traditionally, we talk of capability in terms of being 'ready, willing, and able' – an idea which reputedly originated with the recruitment of sailors in the seventeenth century. To be ABLE is to have skill and knowledge matched to the needs of the job. Such a match requires practised skill and is the normal target of training, best addressed by on-the-job learning, in addition to knowledge gained in the classroom. For our ability to be effectively applied, we need to be READY – to have the capacity to act. Have we the confidence? If we are in a group with others, can we work well together? Can we build mutual respect and trust, to enable us to collaborate? Have we inner fortitude? Such attributes come through practice, through rehearsal, and through exercises of various kinds. Even if these two factors are fulfilled, there remains the question of whether we are WILLING. Will we rise to the occasion, open our eyes to the dangers, and still say 'Yes' to the challenge. This needs courage and vision. Will is developed by response to challenges which start at a modest level and increase rapidly, in pace with development.

I once struck up a climbing partnership with a young man I met in Chamonix. We were both in need of a partner in order that we could venture into the mountains. He spun a good yarn, had all the gear, and was enthusiastic about climbing. I had ambitions to travel the frontier ridge from the summit of Mont Blanc, over Mt Maudit and Mt Blanc du Tacul, eventually descending the Mer de Glas to Montenvers – a wonderful high-altitude expedition, which he bought into. I hiked up to Nid d'Aigle, for the acclimatisation and to save money, while he rode the tramway. We made our way to the Gouter hut for the night, with a plan to be first on the mountain, long before dawn. To my surprise, my colleague was late and slow, so we were almost last to leave, stepping on to the glacier to see a long snake of lights bobbing up the dark snow far ahead.

As we had a serious challenge, I drove us on, passing many of the peak-baggers on this popular tourist route up Mt Blanc. However, once we were high on the mountain, it became clear to both of us that we were out of our depth; his skill was largely theoretical and his confidence was revealed as no more than bravado. His evident struggle with self-doubt and invented excuses for delay had no place in such a serious undertaking. Although he had bought into the intent of our joint enterprise, his lack of capacity made him rightly fearful. Fear further reduced his capacity. The higher we got, the worse it became, until it was impossible for him to proceed. At the Valot hut, faced with mythical frostbite, we abandoned our trip and went our separate ways. The weakness of our relationship, to which my own arrogance had undoubtedly contributed, compromised our joint capacity, so we lacked the capability to safely proceed.

WEIGHING PEOPLE UP

Looking at people, individually or collectively from each of the three per-spectives, gives a richer picture than simply measuring their skill. At High Trenhouse, our small staff (15 people) profile one another on these three parameters in 360 degree assessments. A simple questionnaire gives us a clear picture of our aggregate capability as an organisation. First, people look at how well each person's skills match their job – and whether they need training or experience. Second, they assess motivation and resil-ience, which is often very telling. Little clues enable you to judge whether someone can be relied upon in all situations and what their limitations might be. Do they arrive early and get stuck into work? What is the small talk? Do they have an air of confidence and self-worth? Do they come up with ideas? Are they happy? Third, there is the question of commitment to the purpose. What evidence is there either way? Do they relish challenge? Are they rooting for the next change of game? Can they be relied upon in all conceivable circumstances?

In spite of being very subjective, this exercise provides us all with a very useful impression. Anonymous assessment produces a spread of views, which leads to very fruitful discussions. Differences of perception can be particularly valuable as a trigger to exploration, revealing changes to be embraced. As well as making everyone aware of overall capability and their own contribution, it provides a springboard for personal develop-ment. The team becomes self-aware.

TOWARDS MATURITY

We can surmise that for many people, life experience will balance the aspects of their capability and expand their capability cube, so that they mature.

In the hero's journey, this triad is not made explicit but it is certainly implied; the hero is self-realising! Embarking on the journey requires a kind of awakening – a raising of awareness. Crossing the threshold into the realm of the unknown awakens capacity. Leaving the magical worlds to return home is clearly a question of intent.

For example, Daren* worked for a large consulting firm and came to me as a client, in need of coaching for supposed lack of gravitas. We explored what this might mean in periodic encounters over the ensuing months, during which we developed an excellent relationship. I stretched his imagination using Sufi teaching stories, we videoed him talking, we modelled his issues and his work, we walked over the hills, climbed, and abseiled. We probed his What, How, and Why. Throughout these varied activities, I was able to reflect back to him the way he came across, and he was eager to learn quickly from the feedback. By the time our contract ran out, he had clearly become master of his destiny. What a privilege it is to work with someone in a way that awakens them to their true worth.

Most of us have met people who, though perhaps lacking academic achievement or obvious wealth, have become outstanding human beings. They have a good balance between skill, capacity, and intent. Though their metier might be specific, narrow, or humble (a farmer or a care worker, perhaps) it has taught them to be one, whole, and substantial. Such inner quality spills into every aspect of their living and their work. Despite the system within which they operate, people who become effective teachers and coaches (whether formal or informal) manage to balance the three aspects of learning, to achieve harmonious development of individuals, teams, organisations, or communities. Their capability shines forth as a beacon for all. Their leadership helps make life meaningful.

How different from mainstream education and training, which tends to be satisfied with measurable outputs – of facts retained, skill and knowledge with little regard for capacity or intent. Similarly, in the workplace, for the most part the purpose of training and development is to make people more productive, rather than to realise their human potential. Focus on the measurable neglects those aspects of a person that makes their efforts worthwhile.

The three internal attributes of Why, How, and What, which we have examined in this chapter, signify capability and manifest externally in the way we show up in the world. In the next chapter, we look at how that works and how it affects our actions.

EXERCISE 3: YOUR TRIAD OF BEING AND BECOMING

Thinking about your own inner qualities, how well-developed are you in the different spheres of your life in each of the three parameters; Skill, Capacity, and Intent?

Make a diagram that plots your activities in each domain.

Reflect on:

- How would you like to be?
- What are your aspirations?
- Where are your developmental gaps?
- What are the development opportunities on your diagram?
- What action is required to realise them?

Decide whether you will act!

- If not, why not?
- If not now, then when?

4

Triad of Action

How We Show Up in the World

THE TRIAD FROM ANOTHER VIEWPOINT

In the '90s I was introduced to a framework, related to that in the last chapter, by Charlie Krone, a Californian consultant who built on some of Bennett's ideas and was working at the time with global players such as Dupont and Colgate-Palmolive. He looked at the triad explored in the last chapter from the perspective of how we show up in the world. When we act, our inner attributes manifest through **three kinds of work** – referred to as **OLS**. In terms of 'What,' everyone has **Operations** to perform to which they apply their skill and knowledge. 'How' shows up as the work of influencing the behaviour of others (hence also how you conduct yourself). It brings clarity of meaning and purpose, which increases capacity, and is strongly linked to what we call **Leadership**. 'Why' shows up as **Strategy**, by which people have a grasp of the context in which they will realise their intent.

This is true at every level, from senior positions in large organisations to the lowliest roles – even if you have no formal job, you still show up in these three ways with varying degrees of effectiveness. So, for instance, as an individual I need to do some gardening and shopping as well as attending to work. These are the routine operational activities that fill my days. Leadership relates to those behaviours by which I provide energy, inspiration, encouragement, and support, acting as a model for others. Strategy is where I take the wide and the long view, helping others to do the same – to see the big picture, to dare to dream, to prepare for the unexpected etc. Without strategy, I am no more than a 'leaf at the mercy of the wind.'

I frequently cite the example of the refuse-collectors who serve our centre. They exhibit exemplary operations, performing the task of emptying our bins with great efficiency. Their capacity is manifested in their teamwork: good humour, cooperation, and shared responsibility for the quality of their joint effort. Their intent is clear in that, not only have they a schedule to meet and a goal to return to base with time in hand, but they also do their job with quality and style. These are refuse-collectors and (as is not uncommon) their performance would shame many a senior management team!

ASSESS YOUR OPERATIONS, LEADERSHIP, AND STRATEGY – OLS

Just as in the last chapter, we considered Skill, Capacity, and Intent as an interacting triad, so also their outer manifestation, Operations, Leadership, and Strategy are intertwined and interactive. They flow into one another and any limitations of one will compromise all. Their intensity and degree of integration are what matter and what make all the difference to how well you, your team, your organisation or community perform. It helps to be clear about how you divide your energies between your operational, leadership, and strategic work, so you create a better balance and your energy can be more effectively deployed.

When I work with management teams, I ask people to make a quick sub-jective assessment of how they each divide their time and resources among the three, as a percentage. I note their responses on flipchart for us all to see. It commonly emerges that people are drawn into operational work at the expense of the other two. This is a recipe for becoming very busy, while not getting very good results and feeling overworked. One response is to work even harder – and still not get results – until you get burnout. It is not unusual for managers to say they have 'no time for strategy.' No time for strategy will surely result in no time for anything. And yet every-one has a strategy of some sort. Better that it is conscious and intentional! Strategy addresses the context in which our leadership and operations will realise our aims.

If you then ask people how they would ideally divide their ener-gies among the three, they usually present a different picture, and the

- Organise, prioritise and plan
- Bring about added value results
- Trouble shoot and problem solve
- Monitor results and embrace errors
- Practical work that serves the purpose

OPERATIONS

- Awareness – global and local.
- Develop Purpose, Principles, Policies
- Develop strategic scenarios
- Anticipate threats & opportunities
- Possibility thinking

STRATEGY

- Influence attitudes and commitment
- Motivate, inspire, communicate
- Direct, support and coach
- Clarify what success looks like
- Give and receive feedback

LEADERSHIP

Everyone has three kinds of work

DIAGRAM 4.1
OLS framework

differences suggest how they might choose to change. The three aspects get too readily conflated, which brings confusion and frustration. It also explains why we so often hear the phrase, 'we need to be more strategic.' Just bringing this framework to people's attention can already make their imbalances conscious, and thereby enable them to make improvements.

WHAT DOES IT MEAN IN PRACTICE?

We sometimes run a mock mountain rescue exercise at High Trenhouse. Whatever group is involved, they are unexpectedly asked to be a scratch rescue team and come to the help of a sick person lost on the moors. It is necessary to mount a search on the basis of initially scant information, aiming to quickly get medication to the casualty if they find him. More information comes through as people are spread out in unfamiliar territory with stretched communications. The group picks up clues to the casualty's whereabouts and, as it responds to vague changes, is likely to flounder. They may or may not find the casualty and may or may not have the medication to hand, depending on what they have anticipated in this alien setting. After returning to base the group is required, as part of the exercise, to give a press conference, which gives them an opportunity to put a good spin on whatever outcome they managed to achieve.

A group of senior metropolitan police officers responded very quickly (as they are trained to do) sitting in the Landrover ready for the off within

20 minutes – but with no idea of where to go, because, in meeting their own target response time, they had failed to plan. On the other hand, they did eventually run an excellent press conference (again a function of their training). What a shame that, for lack of strategy, the casualty died!

On a different occasion, one of the rescue team got bored with searching and wandered off sightseeing. The exercise had to be quickly reframed – no longer an exercise but now a real search – we had lost the MD! That told everyone a great deal about the cohesion of the organisation and how, in the absence of leadership or strategy, operations can drift wildly off course.

The point of such exercises is that they give maximum opportunity for cock-ups, because it is by embracing our errors that we learn. We can see things differently when outside our normal metier. However, such exercises should always be reviewed with care and skill, in order to get the most out of them. Ideally, you will have some group memebers whose role is to observe, record, and later provide feedback. More than anything, instead of habitually engaging in blame games (news media are particularly guilty of this) people learn how to learn, and to appreciate the value and process of giving and receiving feedback.

IN THE REAL WORLD

That was 'only an exercise' from which valuable lessons were learned. In the 'real world,' we were asked to assist the senior management of an old textile company to re-form around a newly appointed MD. Although budgetary constraints were challenging, she strongly believed that a focus on development could set them on the road to success. The parent organisation was inclined to run down the operation and eventually close it. This was the company's last chance! There were great challenges on the one hand and, on the other, tremendous potential, that would stretch the capacity of the team as they sought a new way of working. We were asked to design and implement an extended development process to build management capability and develop new levels of success for the company.

In his long tenure, the previous MD employed a ruthless controlling style that had achieved bottom-line results – but at a high price. Senior managers had become disempowered, morale throughout the company was abysmal, and energy had drained away. Endless cost cutting had resulted in deteriorating infrastructure. The weaving shed was draped with plastic in a vain attempt to protect machinery from rain leaking through the Victorian north-light roof. The site was dominated by its chimney – a relic of its steam-driven looms. Despondent groups of workers wastefully trundled materials back and forth from one end of the town to another, because the premises were so dysfunctional. The business was threatened with closure, unless it could be turned around.

WHY A JOURNEY WAS NEEDED

In an initial visit we met the team and appraised the site, its problems, and its people. In meetings with the MD and HR director, we co-designed a highly interactive process of which they shared ownership, committing them to making things happen.

Far-reaching change was needed if the company was to revive. Success depended on the ability of the senior team to envision the kind of company that could thrive in the changed trading environment. A new style of management was required, that could engage the wit, wisdom, and energies of people throughout the company, to develop leadership and strategies that would drive innovative operations. All the management team were committed and keen to embark on the journey.

THE JOURNEY BEGINS

Off-site residential workshops took place at High Trenhouse, an oasis of calm and focus in the Yorkshire Dales. Set in beautiful, unspoiled surroundings, the authenticity and wholeness of the place rubbed off on participants. Having the place to themselves gave them the security to tackle difficult issues. The healing qualities of time in contact with nature, helped people to think and relate creatively.

A holistic principle came into play. The executive team's learning behaviour communicated strongly throughout the organisation, enabling others to view change positively and to collaborate in achieving it. With minimal use of external resources, the leadership learning journey was sustained with periodic interactions while, at the same time, practical changes of structure, infrastructure, and personnel were taking place.

Members of the senior team (and ultimately everyone in the company) learned by doing their work, at the same time as improving their work by continuously learning. The developmental (hero's) journey was paced to match the capacity of the team as they developed their skill, capacity, and intent.

Thus, they showed up and communicated to everyone, through their leadership, strategy, and operational work, as they wrought changes in the organisation. There was a strong sense of caring for every individuals' progress and well-being.

THE RETURN

Over a period of 2 years the company was turned around, from basket case to group exemplar. Enhancements to workflow and the working environment were achieved economically and with very positive impact on morale. As unproductive working practices were removed, frustration and disillusion evaporated, releasing enormous energy. It was like witnessing a sleeping giant awaken. People who had appeared downtrodden and dispirited discovered a new zest for living. Increased effectiveness exposed weaknesses and limitations and, without coercion, those who were unwilling to keep pace with the changes sought their futures elsewhere. Design, production, and quality improved, with the result that the whole financial picture became positive and bright.

A BACKWARD GLANCE

The extended process of development brought a further level of maturity to the organisation and those within it. A strong core team emerged, with a coaching style of leadership which transformed the way of working, from the creaking patterns of 20th century control and command, into something fit to thrive in the new millennium. Engaged and energetic people made steps in personal development and relationship through involvement in leadership and teamwork. Their resilience and adaptability enhanced creativity and innovation, leading to outstanding results. Self-esteem rose to new heights and people were proud of the capability and success they achieved. The organisation strengthened its cohesion, capacity, and effectiveness to become an outstanding commercial success and an exemplar within the parent group.

PSYCHOLOGY OF SUCCESS

What we witnessed in this piece of work, was that, as an organisation inwardly develops its skill, capacity, and intent (SCI), it becomes outwardly effective in its operations, its systemic flow of leadership, and its broad strategies (OLS). As inner and outer grow symbiotically, the people also grow and flourish. This is healthy and wholesome life and work. The difference between dysfunction and thriving is subtle and, for the large part, psychological. What a pity that, in this day and age, we still tend to put so much emphasis on the physical and mechanical aspects of organising.

Let me illustrate this difference with two contrasting stories. In the first, we were called to help an organisation that was taken over by a global player and was struggling to meet demands for enhanced quality and higher productivity. The plant, a glassworks making TV screens, was the major employer in a small town. If jobs were lost the whole community would suffer, so the workers had a huge incentive to tackle the issues. We worked initially with management but there seemed to be blockages. When we spoke to workers, there were some who were prepared to work long hours, without pay if necessary, in order to address the basic issues. Unfortunately, some managers experienced this bold initiative as a threat to their self-importance ('Who do they think they are?') and blocked the move. This triple rejection of the workers; their strategy, their leadership, and even their operational work – resulted in an impasse and ultimately in closure of the plant. Suboptimal output is rarely the fault of either managers or the people they manage – more often the problem lies in the system.

On a happier occasion, we were asked to help the manufacturing subsidiary of a global organization, whose two sites were threatened by closure due to quality issues and poor economic performance. We initially worked off-site with the senior team, who identified a broad range of cultural disjunctions. People with information and ideas were not talking to one another, whereas those who knew what was needed believed it was not their job to act. Organisational structures kept people in functional silos and managers had difficulty seeing that it was their leadership that could bring about changes of attitude and engagement. Nevertheless, as the senior team themselves embraced the need to change, they invited us to run a 1-day workshop with the workforce on each site.

In order to involve the 'whole system,' people were gathered from across divides; functional, geographic, and hierarchical. All had some familiarity with the issues and were asked to externalise the frustrations, problems, and challenges they could think of. Working in small groups they put all their ideas on to MagNotes (hexagonal dry-wipe cards displayed on whiteboards – see next chapter) and clustered them. For each cluster, subgroups envisioned what success would look like in a future with the issues resolved. With these two contrasting pictures in mind, new groups were formed to focus on specific actions to bring about the desired changes. Having 'been to the future,' they were able to see the problems of the current reality from a different and liberating perspective. Cognitive dissonance provided the energy.

A large number of innovation projects emerged within the day and people self-organised into project teams to work on them. 70% were implemented within a month at a negligible cost. The rest followed quickly. It seemed all that had been needed was a well-structured conversation and permission to act. The upshot was cathartic. Huge amounts of energy that had been pent up in frustration was released to directly address the issues that mattered. The business was saved because the managers successfully integrated the Operations, Leadership, and Strategy of the whole organisation.

WHAT MAKES A DIFFERENCE

Key features that contribute to success are:

- The 'whole system' is present and fully engaged.
- The culture of the interventions encourages openness and honesty.
- People are encouraged to imagine what success looks like.
- Issues are explored in a way that presupposes resolution.
- All ideas raised are captured and available for groups to include in their projects.
- People freely choose to join projects for which they have energy.
- People are given power to resolve issues.

A COACHING STYLE OF LEADERSHIP

Those are corporate examples and yet the principles come right down to the scale of our individual way of living. At the start of this chapter, I mentioned my own operations, leadership, and strategic work. Similarly, I look at a colleague and see that he is operationally a very busy person. Because he is preoccupied, he is more inclined to instruct than to influence. It saves him time in the short term, but his leadership is compromised by giving instructions. Of course, he finds it quicker to do things himself than to coach someone else to be able to do them. This, not uncommon situation, can be tackled by delegating more – but delegating needs to be distinguished from abdicating. He knows that, strategically, coaching would give a return on the investment, enabling others to increasingly take initiative and responsibility, until he can delegate. If he could pause and take a look at his OLS, he would surely change his priorities.

And is this really any different from how we bring up our children, coaching them to be able to assume a degree of responsibility while (perhaps reluctantly) giving them independence? We need to work at it, lest we set them up to fail. Although it is unlikely that we would use that language of strategy, leadership, and operations, the same principles apply. Strategically, our offspring need to become self-directing and self-sustaining. Their leadership will inevitably influence and be influenced. Operationally, they need to work, to eat, to live, and to love.

In this chapter, we have explored how the triad of Skill, Capacity, and Intent shows up as action in the world. In the next chapter, we look at the way we think in patterns. We will explore briefly the pattern-making methodology of LogoVisual Thinking – so-called 'algebra of the mind!' We will also take a look at another cyclic phenomenon, Ring Composition, and how it fits with the creative cycle, the triads, and the enneagram.

EXERCISE 4: HOW DO YOU SHOW UP IN THE WORLD?

How do you divide your resources between Operations, Leadership, and Strategy? Think about it, not just in your work but also in how you live your life (if there is any difference).

- Make a chart allocating percentages to each, as you feel them to be, in terms of time or energy, and then as you would like them to be.
- Are you happy that you have the balance right?
- How might you change your priorities to be closer to your ideal?
- What will you do more of/less of, stop doing or start doing so that you can feel you have a better balance?
- How will you know that you have improved?

5

Pattern Thinking

Making Sense and Making Meaning

PATTERN RECOGNITION

We will come across the phenomena of natural cycles again, in a surprising way. In this chapter, we will encounter ring composition – a narrative technique that emerged as we developed LogoVisual Thinking (LVT) methodology. It suggests that somehow our life cycles are reflections of a hidden source of patterning, which our minds can tune into when we commit to pursuing a specific outcome.

Our minds recognize patterns of experience. As infants, we learn to name these patterns, and the naming of patterns of experience gives us our cognitive capabilities. The names we give to objects, processes, and behaviours are the basis of language. Language enables us to think and to communicate, so the recognition of patterns is the key to our understanding. Building ever more complex patterns and constantly updating them are the ways we make sense of the world. For the most part, we position new ideas within the existing complex patterns familiar to our minds (our paradigms). To a limited extent, we rearrange those patterns in order to make better sense of the world, applying unconscious algorithms to decide what is 'truth.' Sometimes new ideas or experiences shatter parts of the patterns in our mind and allow new structures of understanding to emerge.

For developmental purposes, it is useful to differentiate between **making sense** (retrospectively fitting new data into the prevailing patterns in our mind) and **making-meaning** (creatively entertaining an emergent new pattern we can choose to realise). Making meaning is the creation of new worlds. For example, the hiatus of the COVID-19 pandemic creates a space in which many people can sense the opportunity to choose between going back to the old order or reframing in order to create a different society.

Although they sound similar, there is a huge difference. Making sense is the way we interpret the world as we find it. We bring experience into the domain of the familiar by explaining it in terms we understand. Making sense fits experience into our existing paradigms and helps us maintain our sanity. However, in times of major systemic disruption, we will be swamped unless we learn to make meaning. Making meaning is how we shape our future, creating a world that is different from that we inherited – a change of paradigm. Making meaning simultaneously changes the meaning-maker. It is important to differentiate between the two. No amount of sense making will help when macro change is about to engulf you. The popular aphorism about rearranging the deck chairs on the Titanic sums up the difference.

LEVELS OF LEARNING

Hence, we need to be more aware that not all learning is of the same kind. Surprisingly, in business and even in education, there is little appreciation of this. We can usefully reflect on the five levels of learning proposed by that great thinker, Gregory Bateson, based on his anthropological research.

> **LEARNING 0** merely adds to and updates information and knowledge.
> **LEARNING 1** relates to knowing WHAT to do (how to behave) in a known world. It is good for dealing with predictable or repeated situations. Like an instruction manual, it tends to dismiss alternatives in favour of one 'right' answer.
> **LEARNING 2** changes the way we interpret our experience and is vital to our ability to cope with change. Learning 2 changes the learner and how they approach Learning 1 – we learn how to learn. This level of learning is concerned with improving HOW we do what we do, addressing the PROCESS of doing rather than the TASK itself.

To learn at this level, we need to observe, letting go assumptions and attitudes in response to feedback. Chris Argyris called this 'Double-Loop Learning.'

LEARNING 3 involves a further level of abstraction, questioning the WHY of things within a wider context. Such transformative learning shatters both forms and structures, changing our world-view and disrupting who and what we are.

LEARNING 4 is a metalevel that is theoretically possible, but, according to Bateson, unlikely to be present on earth.

Learning 1 is fine for making sense, but making meaning requires Learning 2 and even Learning 3, as it alters the meaning structure of the learner. So, for instance, paradigm shift on a global scale may be a prerequisite for dealing with the consequences of the COVID-19 pandemic, climate change, or economic meltdown. We will all need to embrace change!

CHANGING PATTERNS OF THINKING

When I joined Bennett's Institute for Comparative Study, at Coombe Springs, we took part in many seminars and conversations related to Bennett's research projects. At that time, he was articulating his concept of Systematics – a way of understanding complex systems by viewing them as interactions between different numbers of impulses. So, for instance, one started with the monad – a one-term system which is the undivided whole. It quite soon becomes necessary to consider the internal stresses and contradictions, for which two terms were required; the dyad. A three-term system, the triad, is necessary if one is to think about the dynamics within the system and resolve the conflict inherent in the dyad. The tetrad produces order – and so on, at increasing levels of complexity, right up to 12-term systems.

One significant insight that emerged from this work was that knowledge is structured information. Information without structure is not knowledge. Furthermore, understanding is a grasp of the structure of knowledge. As education aims to impart understanding, we can examine the structures of meaning acquired by a student, so that we test understanding, rather than merely testing retention. This insight was the basis of a project Bennett's group worked on for General Electric Company (GEC), to develop remote tutoring (i.e., what came to be called 'teaching machines,' before the days of personal computers or even electronic calculators). An initial challenge was for the tutors to understand their own structures of meaning. This involved mapping the structure of one's subject matter, using cards spread on the floor. Later, it evolved into using magnetic hexagons on whiteboards. This technique was later adopted and adapted by Hodgson and Myers (members of the project group) in their work as management consultants.

We used the tools in the early days at High Trenhouse and in the late 1980s. I worked for Hodgson, refining products, writing guides, developing software, and marketing the method. Later, with help from Anthony Blake (another project group member), we evolved the methodology under the name of LogoVisual Thinking (LVT).

LogoVisual Thinking

Beyond problem-solving, mapping the patterns of our knowing is useful for exploring topics of mutual interest in ways that encourage co-creation and collaboration. To the usual advantages of visual thinking, LVT adds motility of ideas. People physically handle and mould their thinking process, which helps them to embrace differences of experience and perception (hence resolution of conflict leads to creative outcomes). As they appreciate that they can cocreate, they find richer relationships and closer alignment. It helps them value diversity, frees them from either–or thinking and leads towards integration of differences.

So, here is a simple description of the process.

1. **Focus:** Alone or with colleagues, you define a topic to explore and post it in the form of a key question that everyone agrees as the focus for enquiry.
2. **Gather:** Let's say you are using sticky notes. Everyone independently writes down their own responses as complete yet succinct statements (actor + verb + object). Ideally, they use bold marker pens and print clearly, so anyone can easily read what is written. Such work requires individual focus and generally inhibits conversation. Discussion is misplaced at this stage, as there is no need for agreement, which simply reduces diversity. When everyone is done, they make a random shared display, taking care that everyone understands what each other has written.

3. **Organize:** Now they can move the items, organizing the material they have cocreated in a way that makes sense to them – usually forming clusters of related ideas. This stage tends to involve lots of conversation, as subtleties of meaning and location get sorted out. The relative positioning of ideas is discovered to be itself significant in discovering meaning.

4. **Epitomize:** Next, they title each cluster with a statement that epitomizes the cluster content. An epitome is also a complete statement (actor + verb + object) – an abstraction that stands for all of the detail it summarizes, capturing also the meaning implied by the physical relationship.

5. **Integrate:** When ready, the epitome titles can be transferred to new sticky notes on a new surface, leaving behind the detail in order to explore the higher-level relationships between the clusters. In effect, people can now begin to view their topic as a system, thereby getting an overall grasp of its internal structure (a systems diagram). Stepping back from the detail encourages metacognition – a shift to a higher level of abstraction.

Of course, some aspects of LVT will be familiar from other methods: For instance, it looks a bit like brainstorming; a bit like Soft-System Modelling; a bit like Institute of Cultural Affairs' Technology of Participation (all of which have their virtues, although they are often conducted rather mechanistically, which weakens their effectiveness). LVT applies a degree of rigor and has something more that is unique and valuable. Precise use of language, disciplined patterning, the hard work of epitomizing, and then add the magic of narrative and the aesthetics of Ring Composition (description to follow) and you produce 'algebra of the mind.' It changes the way people think and how they relate. Instead of compromise, people transcend disagreement, using minimal facilitation – the people effectively do it themselves! Surprisingly quickly, a group can arrive at a shared understanding. They develop a sound epistemological foundation on which to plan or decide.

As Gregory Bateson wrote (*Angels Fear*, pg. 152),

> Structure is the algebra of that which is to be described; It is always one degree more abstract. Structure presumes a gathering and sorting of some of the infinite details, which can then be thrown away and summary statements offered in their place.

WHAT THE METHODOLOGY ENABLES YOU TO DO WELL

Whereas the LVT methodology can be useful when working solo, it is especially valuable when you want to achieve richer results by pooling the diverse perspectives of a group. It is scalable because it is easy to merge outputs from different groups, so a hundred people can engage in a single thinking process with great effectiveness. LVT has proved successful in school rooms, for individual work, with management teams at all levels, and for community groups addressing widely varying challenges. It encourages exploration, allowing groups to rapidly gather richly diverse input.

LVT enables you to:

- Create new structures of thinking including all contributions without rejection.
- Use disaggregation and reaggregation to shake up old structures of meaning.
- Change levels of perception to achieve well-informed high-quality results.
- Guide the process without influencing the content.

All this may sound a bit highfalutin, but it is really very simple to do. Many schoolteachers use it to help their classes into self-organised exploration of what might otherwise appear to be a complex topic. I have used it with groups sized from one individual to 200. Even illiterate or otherwise handicapped people have been able to participate, because it is a naturally collaborative thinking process.

LVT PROCESS AND THE DIFFERENCE
THAT MAKES A DIFFERENCE

Usually, in brainstorming, a facilitator notes down ideas, randomly generated by a group, which are later evaluated. Although the random ideation is similar, LVT demands a more rigorous approach. In small groups of no more than five people (larger numbers work in parallel subgroups), participants write their own ideas, concisely and precisely, that is, brief yet complete statements with an active verb and an object. Each idea is written on a separate card, so it can be manipulated independently.

The facilitator stands back, as people pool their material and organise it into clusters, rather than categories. Categorisation sorts information according to similarity, primarily so we can retrieve it by following logical trees – as in a filing system. To cluster ideas is to intuitively differentiate (sometimes putting together conflicting ideas) with the aim of breaking free from past logic to allow novelty to emerge.

Instead of merely naming the clusters, in LVT, we epitomise their content. This is a significant part of the process of meaning-making. The epitome is also a full statement with a verb, which must stand for the detail contained in the cluster when that detail is left behind. Writing an epitome can be challenging, because it needs to sum up all the content of the cluster. Producing epitome titles instead of labels elevates thinking to *a higher logical level*. Freed from being bogged down in detail, working with epitomes, you can address the overall structure, untying whatever cognitive Gordian knots might have been causing dysfunction. As participants explore how these high-level concepts relate, they gain the understanding which can help them resolve their issues.

The exercise at the end of this chapter will enable you to discover the elegant (hard won) simplicity of this process.

Where participants have worked as subgroups (unless they have been working on different topics), there will be a need to combine outputs. We could choose to do this by pooling all the separate ideas, but it is more easily done when we use only the epitomes, leaving behind the detail. In the process, it might be desirable to do some second-order clustering of epitomes, if there are overlaps, taking care not to cluster together items from any one subgroup (not putting together what they had differentiated). Simple colour-coding makes this straightforward.

According to your process, you will be aiming for 7–15 epitomes. This higher-level material can then be structured as a conventional systems diagram, looking for sequences, cause–effect relationships, and feedback loops, so you reveal the system's internal dynamics. More potently, a narrative technique – ring composition – will enable you to move to a yet higher logical level of integration and abstraction. This epistemological process facilitates the creation of new meaning.

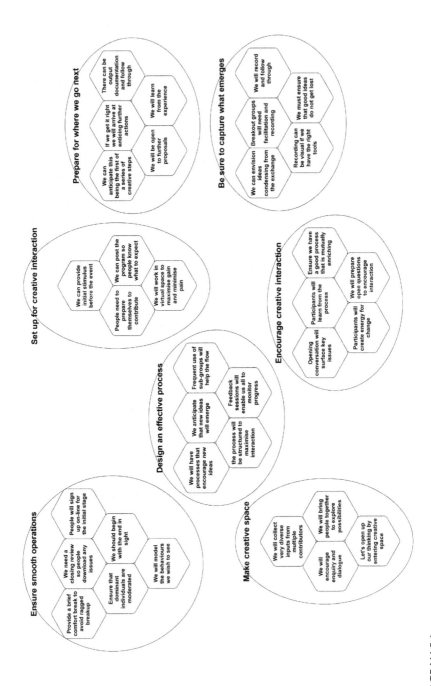

DIAGRAM 5.1

Design for an online workshop – clusters and epitomes

RING COMPOSITION

Ring composition is a narrative that ends where it begins, reminiscent of the hero's journey. In Chapter 7, we will look at a practical example. It is usually conducted as a whole-group interactive exercise. Having created the 7–15 epitomes as described, someone chooses which epitome will be the start of the narrative and then proceeds from there to create a ring that works as a narrative, perhaps not getting very far to begin with. The facilitator will encourage others to try alternative starts and sequences. Sometimes, it pays to work backward from the end. Usually, each person's attempt is captured (a digital photograph), so that it is possible to backtrack, if necessary. After much conversation and experimentation, the group will arrive at a narrative that includes all of their epitomes and tells a story that is acceptable to everyone. Then, they can apply an aesthetic test (Yes! aesthetics of thinking!).

Referring to the structure of ring compositions, the facilitator asks people to identify the latch and the turn. Then, drawing horizontal lines between pairs, they are invited to check for a correspondence between the outward journey and the return. There may well be a need for some adjustments. Perhaps repositioning one or two of the elements or even moving the ring on its axis will make it 'feel' better. At some point, it should

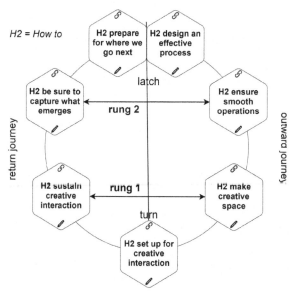

DIAGRAM 5.2
Design for an online workshop – ring composition.

achieve a satisfying aesthetic – it will seem beautiful. When that beauty is achieved, someone can 'read' the story aloud as a last check on its credibility with those who created it.

STRATEGIES

The story may be hugely satisfying in itself (it often wins a round of applause) and is valuable in helping turn concepts into strategies as we prepare for action. In the next stage, we allocate the rungs to individuals and have them write a new epitome to reconcile the tensions between the outward and return ends of their rung (a dyad). Whereas a fishbone (Ishikawa) diagram is most often used to analyse causes of a problem, here we reverse its function, in order to discover causes that we can put in place to achieve a desired outcome.

For each rung, position the new epitome at the head end of the spine, as the future outcome of a strategy. At the tail end, summarise the relevant current

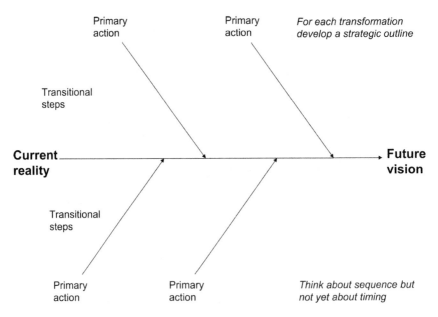

DIAGRAM 5.3
Design for an online workshop – fishbone

reality. Add ribs for each transition that is required to drive the total transformation from current reality to ideal outcome. Add details of required actions. A neat trick is to plot these as 'How-to's' (H2s). For example, 'H2 make sure our quality surpasses client expectations' will be a more effective stimulus to creativity than saying, 'Deal with quality issues.'

Subgroups can now cross-present, so that everyone gains an understanding of the strategies outlined for each of the rungs. When they share the full picture, they will be better able to progress the details in order to produce plans and actions. Such a session should close with looking at next steps, which will specify what will be done in the short term, by whom, by when, in order that momentum is maintained. It will wrap up with a review of the whole process, so any concerns can be noted, and no learning lost.

LVT HAS WIDE APPLICATIONS

LVT has applications wherever people need to explore challenging issues and complex problems. For half a century, it has been used to excellent effect: management teams addressing business planning, community groups thinking about future needs, and students researching their theses. Instead of absorbing meaning structures from the past, people are differentiating and integrating ideas in order to make new meaning and achieve shared outcomes. With LVT, we make connections between fragments of wisdom and experience. By disassembling our diverse experience and pooling the parts, we can gain freedom from our mental boundaries. From the gathered items, we identify new groupings and consider afresh how they interrelate to form new patterns of meaning. Rigor of language in place of casualness, clustering in place of categorising, epitomising in place of labelling, integration in place of sorting, all differentiate LVT from other methods. Such thinking has the potential to change the world we live in by changing the way we perceive it. It pushes us to think at higher levels of abstraction, brings people into relationship, makes learning fun, and develops capability.

The important thing for this book is that LVT can help us make meaning in a way that transforms us – furthering, in effect, our hero's journey and liberating the flow of leadership.

A PROVOCATION AND A SCAFFOLD
TO EXPLORE MORE DEEPLY

We should note that there is a correspondence between the enneagram framework, the hero's journey, and ring composition – the basic cyclic pattern of life. The words used differ slightly from one framework to another, but the quality of the structure is consistent, whether we are dealing with cooking, with personal, social, or corporate issues, with hero's journeys, or life-cycles. There is no right or wrong to any of it and no simple formula – just a provocation to think more deeply and search for understanding. As you begin to explore and use such structures, the quality of your thinking will be enriched, enabling you to think more in terms of organic wholeness, as a counterbalance to our inherited tendency to think in reductionist fragments.

BOX 5.1 DEVELOP YOUR PATTERNING CAPABILITY

Get a pad of sticky notes and a bold pen.

Decide on a topic for enquiry. Typically, imagine some future desirable state of affairs. Imagine that it has been realised, i.e. that the future already exists, so you write about it **in the present tense**.

> For example, 'It is 3 years since I did this exercise. Now I have remodelled my garden so that I can enjoy using it to entertain friends and family.'

Describe your future success in as much detail as you can. Write each of your responses on a separate note; make each a full statement with an active verb (not a gerund).

Stick with your enquiry for half an hour, aiming to produce 20–40 responses.

When you have exhausted your experience and imagination, review your results and look for what ideas fit most closely together. Start with pairs and then let them grow. As you move them around, form clusters of no more than six or seven items. Try to cluster rather than to categorise (I leave you to reflect on the difference).

Write EPITOMES for each cluster; a full statement, with a verb, that stands for all the contained items, such that no meaning is lost if the contents are removed. Do this with rigor – this is meaning-making. This is a very important step which we discovered in LVT, but other methods tend to overlook, resulting merely in simplification rather than in integration.

Copy your epitomes onto new sticky notes and, working now at this more abstract level (leaving aside the detail) explore the dynamic relationship between your clusters, as a systems diagram. You could then duplicate the epitomes and see whether you can produce a ring composition. However, this may be too ambitious without practice, colleagues, or skilled facilitation.

Reflect on:

- What new insights have you generated about the question?
- Are you aware of developing a broader perspective?
- Do you see changes in your understanding?

6

Self-Organisation

Leadership and Teamwork

LEADERSHIP IS POWER TO NOT, POWER OVER

Back in the '80s, people in organisations used to argue over whether they were managers or leaders. It seemed that management and leadership were alternatives or that one might start out as a manager and then become a leader. When you think about those distinctions in today's context the surprising conclusion is that, although it is nice when managers exhibit leadership, leadership can appear anywhere in an organisation (or outside it). It seems that, in an organic organisation, leadership is nothing other than a flow of energy between people, to which all can contribute.

The old definitions confuse leadership with power. Powerful people are often called leaders, even though they tend to manage rather than lead, because power gives them control. The flow of energy can, to some extent, be controlled (or usurped) by power. The downside of such an approach is that power, in Newtonian terms, can evoke an equal and opposite reaction. People can freely choose to contribute to a flow of energy but, under compulsion, may withdraw their contribution or even actively resist. Mainstream leadership development focuses on techniques by which power can manipulate people to serve its own ends. Furthermore, leadership is positioned as what 'leaders' do, identifying the role with the particular power-possessing person. This very common idea about the nature of leadership, which is often exploitative and cynically manipulative, is dangerous and damaging. It disempowers the majority of people and undervalues their potential. This disparity between perception and reality has been highlighted during the COVID-19 pandemic, where we have seen many instances of the impotence of the power-possessing and the potency of the unacknowledged heroes of the service sector.

LEADERSHIP AND SELF-ORGANISATION

An alternative, wholesome view of leadership is that everyone can, must, and undoubtedly does make leadership contributions – indeed that the flow of energy we call leadership occurs most effectively when there is a quality of relationship that engages everyone involved. The overall flow is guided, or drawn forth, by a shared sense of purpose. Individuals step into and out of the stream of leadership as and when appropriate, according to who can see most clearly, who has energy to act, and who has the requisite strength, as well as who has the right skills for the situation. Different requirements are met by different people as events unfold. The unfolding depends upon mutual trust and respect enabling open relationships to flourish.

Self-organisation is at odds with the conventional concept of leadership. If anyone attempts to control, self-organisation is automatically displaced. Self-organisation is best experienced directly through work, although many people need to play together to get the flavour of it. This is, for instance, the usual purpose of off-site experiential retreats, as a result of which groups of all sizes can work and play together to co-create a leadership flow within their organisation.

I have always enjoyed the feeling of euphoria when a group, of which I was a part, excelled in some way. I enjoyed climbing mountains and working on architectural projects because in both the activities, I experienced peaks of performance. It usually involved risk or danger and sometimes challenged me and my various different colleagues to the extreme. Yet, it was invariably worthwhile. Why? Well, I know that on those occasions, I personally exceeded what I thought I was capable of. In other words, through the intensity of the experience I participated in something that was beyond my normal capability. Because I became part of a greater whole, it was transformative!

Having had a later career in helping management teams to perform well, I would now say that those formative experiences of mine were to do with co-creation and self-organisation. What started as playful interpersonal dynamics became self-development, team-development, and leadership interactions. By striving to succeed, we learned to be.

As a group of half-dozen young men, we set out to traverse the Grepon, a needle of rock in the Mont Blanc massif. Although it is very steep and airy, it is not a particularly difficult climb. However, our large party was slow. As we approached the summit spire, on the other side of which we would commence our descent, we were overtaken by a thunderstorm, with lightning striking nearby peaks. The rocks around us began to howl eerily with the electricity passing through them. As the first on the rope arrived on the summit, he received an electric jolt and quickly withdrew. Fortuitously, we found a crevice in the precipitate rocks in which to shelter for the night that was now upon us. We all managed to squeeze into its narrow protection and my back formed the door, shutting out the storm. With scant provisions and very little sleep, we were relieved that the morning brought clear blue skies. Breaking our ropes free from the icy rocks, we were able to cross the summit and descend safely. In our leaderless group, the decision-making was dispersed but effective. Moreover, we learned to be more prepared for adverse weather and aware of the need to move faster.

TOWARDS WHOLENESS

This is how we might discover the wholeness of teams – a quality of relationship between people. In so far as we share a common purpose, we can be more aware of our individuality, allowing it to be subsumed into the shared identity of the team. Because it enables us to transcend our usual limitations, being a part of a high-performing team is profoundly different from just being one of a group. It depends upon individuals choosing to become part of something larger than themselves. I have seen this work with social groups, with junior and senior teams and whole departments, with partnerships and conglomerates. Using quite short and intensive interactions, both off-site and at work, imagination and commitment enable people to devise processes that get breakthrough results.

PROCESSES AND METHODS FOR CO-CREATION

There are processes and techniques that enable groups of disparate individuals to meet, to pool their expertise and ideas, to find common ground, and design novel outcomes for all manner of purposes and at any scale – from family groups to management teams and from community initiatives to international collaborations of global significance. Without any overt control, it is possible for such groups to achieve phenomenal outcomes. Indeed, it sometimes happens that the foregoing of control structures allows people to achieve better results much more efficiently. If this is true, then a systematic cataloguing of these processes and techniques would surely be worthwhile.

I have seen co-creation work in organisations, where layers of management (and 'supervision') became unnecessary because people could perfectly well organise themselves, provided they had a clear sense of direction. Not only is unnecessary cost eliminated and the quality and effectiveness of work greatly enhanced, but also people feel powerful and free.

Of course, those with a vested interest in the status quo might be expected to resist. For example, we were at one time involved with helping a community group run various public consultations. The group was ready and willing to tackle major local issues and was excited to be engaged in co-creation. Unfortunately, as a condition of funding, we were required to accept high-powered consultancy help, whereupon all initiative evaporated. The consultants pocketed enough public funding to have covered the cost of the changes we aimed for. We were left with nothing more than a slim report, in which they told us what we had told them! The whole funding exercise was counterproductive and left the community dispirited. Bottom up initiative cannot be driven top down! Self-organisation cannot be organised.

SELF-ORGANISATION AND TEAMWORK

At the heart of self-organisation is the idea of creativity, which is encouraged by rich communication and interaction. Although it is in some ways democratic, self-organisation is much more, because it does not depend on hierarchical structures or mechanisms of democracy (such as representation or voting) in order for people to work together to bring their ideas into reality.

Process of self-organisation incorporating Tuckman's stages of team development

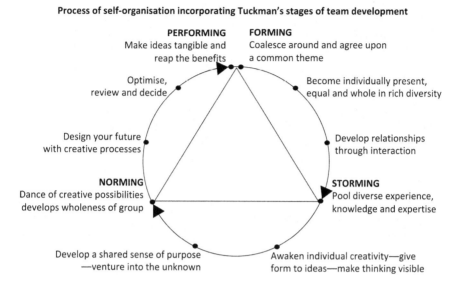

DIAGRAM 6.1
Process of self-organisation

Here is a sketch of the stages of process required for self-organised co-creation.

I have included Tuckman's well-researched 'stages of team development' to hint at the different behaviours you might observe – the process is not linear and not plain sailing – more likely discontinuous and iterative. As you might expect, this framework approximates to the enneagram and also to the hero's journey. In addition, there is a fractal relationship; individuals become more integrated and whole as they participate in a group coming together in performance. The wholeness of the group transcends personal capability: the group as a whole, as well as each of its participants, matures symbiotically. At the scale of the individual and the collective, wholeness comes about, manifesting as an emergent capability beyond that of the parts.

THE OVERALL PATTERN MAKES MEANING

When they subscribe to some cause beyond themselves, their shared sense of purpose brings people into relationship. Then, as they work towards that elected purpose, they mature as a group and each one matures as an individual. The sense of purpose gives meaning to all who are engaged in it, unifies them in shared identity, and helps align them with shared intent, as one living whole. When this happens, we may find the whole is more than the sum of its parts – new capabilities emerge.

I remember one time, in the Alps on an extended trip, I teamed up with an acquaintance I only knew as Matey, to climb the North face of L'Aiguille d'Argentiere. We knew little of each other but shared a spirit of adventure and an appreciation of style. The climb was a snow and ice route – spectacular but not difficult. As dawn broke, fresh and rosy fingered, we ran out long leads (a measure of mutual trust). We were in our metier and enjoyed the sheer freedom of absolute confidence in ourselves and in one another. At one point, I led an awkward icy pitch and was surprised and amused when Matey fell off below me, dangling briefly above a long drop before he regained his footing. It seems absurd, but we were so confident that this little incident only made us laugh. This was a successful two-man team – but then, two is easier than more!

Another teamwork experience I found especially enjoyable was when we were asked to organise a Transatlantic Environment Conference, TRAEC 2000. We gathered a small team of facilitators and technical staff to bring a disparate group of specialists into creative relationship. Our facilitation made use of LVT and we posted the outcomes on to the Internet in real time – quite an achievement in 2000! All this required people to work through the night, in order to be ready once more for the daytime role. Great sacrifices, utterly selfless and professional teamwork involving countless problem-solving exercises, improvisations, challenges, all completed on time! Nobody was 'in charge' and yet everyone knew that whatever was needed to be done, would be done to the very limits of everyone's capability. I have had similar experiences with other large events, when the enabling and support team wholly identified with the needs of participants, wholeheartedly providing the service(s) required. In the COVID-19 pandemic, there have been countless examples of such self-organised achievement in the caring and support services – far beyond the call of duty or what would normally be expected.

_____

TEAM ROLES

Wholeness requires that a team has all the attributes it needs to achieve its ends. When you are involved in collaborative work, it can be quite difficult to differentiate between the technical role you play and a quite different role you have in relation to the team and its members. For a successful process, all technical inputs must be fulfilled, as also must be all the necessary interpersonal dynamics.

When we are doing a project single-handedly, we play all roles in the creative cycle. However, more complex projects involve other people. Different strengths (hence, different people) come into their own at different parts of the cycle. Ideally, as we build a team, we gather a diversity of people to cover all the roles required to successfully accomplish our work, *in addition to technical contributions*. By mapping the role preferences of all team members on to the creative cycle, we can be aware of the strengths and weaknesses of the team as a whole. Any shortfall will need to be addressed, either by recruiting additional talents or by training people to fill the gaps, or perhaps, simply by raising awareness so that the team can compensate for any omissions.

As we saw in Chapter 2, the nine team roles identified by Dr Meredith Belbin in his research at Henley, map on to the creative cycle (as shown below in brackets). Note, Belbin's names tend to suggest individuals, but actually these are simply roles, all of which need somehow to be played between whatever number of players are in the team.

Awareness (Specialist)

Maintaining awareness of the context in which the team is operating, to highlight dangers and opportunities, to raise aspirations, and find fitting challenges. In business, this might fall largely to the business development manager or the entrepreneur. In some cases, the role may fall to a technical specialist.

Exploration (Resource Investigator)

Gathering information, without which we cannot create, requires a talent for discovery; curiosity to look outside the familiar territory for relevant information and make new connections. Finding out what we do not know.

Definition (Team Worker)

Clarifying the task at hand. Maintaining calm and reason to steady those who would be swept away by enthusiasm. Convergent thinking can appear dull to some, in the context of creativity, but no progress will be made without rational decision-making.

Cohesion (Coordinator)

Developing and maintaining the relationships required to succeed when many forces conspire to pull them all apart. Awareness of the whole process and the whole team helps overcome temporary setbacks and reminds people of their mutual commitment.

Ideation (Plant)

Producing a rich variety of ideas. Where one idea might do for others, this talent will keep generating more. The downside is the difficulty in settling for any particular idea and actually progressing in the job. This may exasperate some.

Optimisation (Monitor Evaluator)

There is a need to select, integrate, and present the best of all the possibilities. Done rightly, the parts gel as one whole. This role anticipates the challenges of implementation and pitches the solution, so as to get buy-in and commitment.

Intent (Implementor)

Develops commitment or focuses the collective will on a specific outcome. Weighs major factors and drives for decisions in relation to a wider context. Takes account of the strategic picture, measures risk, and musters total commitment to realising the project.

Action (Shaper)

Ensures that something happens as a result of all the cognitive processes that have gone before. Gets on with the job, helping those on the ground to give their best. Overcomes technical difficulties and delivers on the creative promise by determination and example.

Completion (Completer Finisher)

Works at bringing things to a successful conclusion and final completion, making sure the promise is fulfilled, that everything works, and all is clean and tidy. Commissions systems and tests things out. Wants to see order, quality, and delight in the final result.

Sequenced and mapped on to the Creative Cycle, these give us the following 'radar' presentation, where the concentric circles represent Belbin scores on each parameter – that is, the amount of contribution an individual makes to a particular role. That we are all different, means a team can be composed so that all roles are well covered – as long as team members respect and appreciate each other's different perspectives and contributions. Weak areas can be covered when we are aware of them. This is trickier than it sounds, as we are liable to under-appreciate or even deride the value of roles and behaviours we do not ourselves embrace.

Overlaying individual maps gives an immediate impression of the overall strengths and weaknesses of a particular team, in relation to its primary task. Being able to relate the roles to the creative cycle helps us understand why those roles are necessary and how they relate to one another, clarifying where teams may need to develop or to recruit additional capability. Remember that the red triangle of awareness, cohesion, and commitment refers to states of being rather than actions.

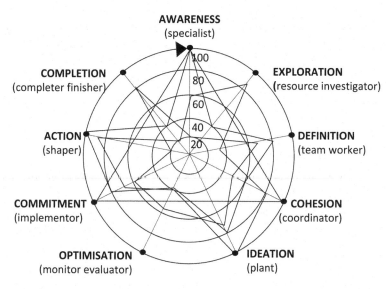

DIAGRAM 6.2
Example profiles of a small team

CO-CREATION AND SELF-ORGANISATION

These roles will be played, whether or not we are aware of them. However, awareness and mutual respect may enable them to be played more consciously and to better effect. Where a group is able to cover the whole process with consistent quality, it has the potential to be self-organising. For that to come about, there must be a free flow of information and energy between the players rather than any hierarchy of power. People will play those roles as and when required, stepping into role and out, according to who is best able to see the way.

Self-organising for co-creation is a social and self-development capability that has largely been overlooked in the organisational world. Self-interest and financial gain have fed a system of power and control which might appear to be 'just the way it is.' It does not need to be like that! Perhaps the hiatus of a pandemic will enable us to show that a more organic and holistic way of being is not only possible but is more wholesome and fulfilling?

LEADERSHIP AS FLOW

In my own work, I have seen that leadership is more subtle than the personal traits that most leadership development aims to encourage in people so they can become 'leaders.' I have seen leadership sparking off in teams, quite independently of who was supposed to be 'the leader.' Leadership can simply flow between people and everyone can contribute to it in some way or another. The flow is a flow towards the shared purpose. The shared purpose provides a context of meaning for all actions. 'Work' becomes meaningful as it aligns with the flow.

It seems the language we use prevents this from being visible to most people, because language presumes that leadership is what leaders do and therefore only people entitled 'leader' can do it. Too often the idea is confused with power. And yet, everyone certainly provides leadership (whatever they call it) in some aspect of their lives. It is present in every transaction between people; in families and communities and all relationships. Unfortunately, too few people take the opportunities they have for leadership in their everyday lives. Perhaps they fear the responsibility they think will follow or, with false modesty, leave such work to others.

What really matters is that we all learn from the many available examples of high-performing teamwork, successful social communities, and exceptional leadership initiatives. Then we can apply our understanding to larger groupings; organisations, communities, and whole societies, so that we promote self-organisation, i.e., self-directed and effective individuals working in relationship. That will enable people to avoid the danger and tyranny of command and control that is inherent in our system. Where it rules, we meekly abdicate responsibility, allowing a self-selected few to fill the void, thus gaining power, which invariably corrupts, robbing us all of meaning.

In this chapter, we have explored the dynamics of self-organisation and teamwork, including the roles that need to be played for people to bond effectively. We have seen how our leadership enables energies to flow. In the next chapter, we will consider the self-organising capability that comes about through clarity of purpose and values. As we saw when we looked at worlds of perception, purpose and values are at a high level of abstraction. If we are not clear there, we are likely to experience conflict in everyday life and dissipate our energies.

EXERCISE 6 EXPLORE: YOUR EXPERIENCE
OF SELF-ORGANISING RELATIONSHIPS

Make notes to yourself of the times when you have experienced a high level of collaboration with others – when something has worked out particularly well.

What were the pinnacles of those experiences? Describe your very best experience of peak performance.

- What preceded it?
- What contributed to it?
- Why do you remember it?
- What made it exceptional?

When you look at that experience, where was the leadership? How did the leadership impinge on your own behaviour? Who displayed leadership? Was it one person or several? How did you respond to someone else's leadership? Did you find yourself, however briefly, providing leadership to anyone else?

7

Clarity of Vision

Strategies for Success

STRATEGY AS NARRATIVE

With clear vision and values, we can be strategic. From our vision, we can produce plans that lead to effective action. When we come to Chapter 8, we will see how a 'Sense of Purpose' sets a direction and establishes a meaning-field. Purpose frames visions and visions frame what can be accomplished within the field determined by the purpose. Vision is more concrete, so it pays to be clear of your purpose before you set about visioning as described in the current chapter.

All our experience is of the past and past experience can certainly help enrich our future. However, it can also severely restrict it, unless we are able to break free from past conditioning. For that, visions can be powerful tools. From visions, strategies can be developed or, more accurately, with vision we can be strategic. Unless we are consciously attempting to invent the future, we may only be capable of reacting to what happens. Great strategists span a wider view of time and space. Their leadership stories inspire belief, raise hope, and change the level of thinking.

Strategy, as narrative, gives scope for every aspect of intelligence – emotional, intellectual, physical, and aspirational. Strategic narratives provide a foundation of meaning. Because they engage the whole person, they enable people to respond well to changes going on around them.

As a former architect, I have been accustomed to visualising the spatial arrangements of clients' operations and then creating the spaces to accommodate them. My strong imagination can also be a nuisance, especially in conversion work, because I can easily be carried away by all the potential I see, sometimes failing to take due account of the difficulty in achieving it. Where a realist will see dereliction and cost, I may be imagining people enjoying beautiful spaces and good living! But how is it to come about?

Architects think broadly in time and space. Nevertheless, it was not until I was embarked upon the High Trenhouse venture that I discovered the power of a vision. I had submitted carefully considered plans for the change-of-use and redevelopment of our broken-down farmstead. Our last pennies were invested in the project. We were living hand-to-mouth on the premises and totally committed. Then, we got the news that planning permission was refused. I recall the feeling of despondency as my wife and I took a walk along a nearby road and her saying, 'You have a strong vision – fight for it!.' That was the first time in my life that I had ever known that I had a vision. It was a revelation – and it was our salvation! We struggled with planning issues repeatedly, for more than a decade as the project came to life, and it was vision that sustained us.

VISION – BACK FROM THE FUTURE

Developing a vision is an exercise in right use of imagination. We can learn to articulate our vision as a description of what success looks like, as if we were there, in some future time. By imagining future success, we greatly increase the possibility of making it real. With a clear vision, we can work back from the future to identify themes, sequences, and pathways that will bring the vision into reality. Then, we can broad-brush strategies that get us from where we are now to where we want to be. While visioning, we have no need to concern ourselves with HOW desired results are to be achieved, because doing so inhibits our imagination. By the same token, we use our imagination to make a leap into the future, so that we are not constrained by incrementalism.

Our strategic intentions will be moderated by our values, so a further exercise will be needed to clarify the values we choose to use as our guide.

Involving the whole system (at whatever scale is appropriate) – not just managers or planners, but, for example, folk from the production workface and those with customer contact – harnesses everyone's engagement, commitment, and passion. To achieve this, we need not just 'a meeting' but rich cultural interaction, ideally including art, drama, stories, dialogue, and serious play, to feed the process. Reversing the idea of 'cascading' strategies down the hierarchy (top-down), developing a strategic narrative integrates multiple contributions into a coherent whole (bottom-up – or better still, on the level). The unifying factors are common purpose, shared values, clarity of vision, and trust in people to do a good job. Then, when it comes to realisation, everyone can live the strategy, aligned in everything they contribute.

Every vision process will be unique, so I will describe some typical processes which enabled visions to be developed. Although the core process can be compressed, a group vision exercise should take at least a day, ideally with an overnight stay. Two days and two nights together will be even better. Apart from the work of putting the imagery of vision into words, there needs to be time for self-discovery and for relationships to deepen, so that ownership is truly shared. A shared vision will richly repay all the resources dedicated to its generation.

You will not find it difficult to scale the typical core process from 1 to 100 people, even though organising around that core will differ greatly. A shorter time may suffice in simple cases, but it is wise to ensure there is enough time for the whole process to run its course. The point is, that a good process not only enables people to clarify their vision, but also prepares them to be better able to realise it. There is a dual benefit – as a team articulates its vision it becomes a better team!

AN INDIVIDUAL EXAMPLE

As individuals, we may need to work on vision when faced with a challenge. For example, Peter was very worried about how he was going to cope with a threat of redundancy. I could see that, unless he could rise to the challenge, his negative thoughts would be a self-fulfilling prophecy. I set him up to work solo and he eventually found a spot on a riverbank where he spent most of the day on his own, refreshments provided! We talked about his needs and aspirations, for which he did a radar plot on flipchart, highlighting where he felt he was and where he would like to be. Then he moved to visioning what success would look like in 5 years – well beyond the redundancy horizon! He gathered ideas on to Magnotes, clustered, and epitomised. He used the epitomes to make a systems diagram, which enabled him to write a narrative statement of what success would look like for him. This was decidedly upbeat and moved him from despondency to confidence in his capacity to thrive on the crisis. He slept on it at the end of a day well spent!

COMMUNITY REGENERATION

A crisis occurred in our local community. Pressures of change were being felt – tourist pressure, rising property prices, falling incomes, agricultural change, and the final blow was when foot-and-mouth disease closed the countryside to visitors. Local people were fragmented, each group with their own concerns, but all were now threatened by crisis. We decided we could use our experience to help our community clarify a way forward. Everyone was invited to the village hall for a workshop and around 60 people showed up – a significant proportion of the population of our deeply rural area.

The hall was prepared so as to be warm and welcoming – table groups, tablecloths, flowers, refreshments, music. People were greeted personally on arrival and invited to post their hopes for the event on a display. The formal process began by identifying all the people who had a stake in the future of the community. Of course, this turned out to be very many – children, relatives, tradespeople, tourists, businesses, local authorities, and so on. The full list of stakeholders went up on the wall for all to see. Although it took only a few minutes, it was valuable to get people to see beyond their own self-interested concerns.

We were able to focus on vision, because, given the crisis, the community desperately needed to find confidence in its future – purpose enough for the time being. So now, we set about externalising all we could imagine as indicators of future success, seeing ourselves enjoying life, and thriving. We used LVT as described in Chapter 5, with a few people in the role of facilitators wandering among the groups to guide people in what they were doing (the novelty of the medium – playing with executive toys – helped free up the thinking).

Ideas were gathered and clustered, epitomes were drafted, and groups cross-presented. Each group transferred their epitomes to larger sticky notes, around half a dozen per group, and clustered them with others on a large sheet of paper stuck to the wall. Epitomes of these second-order clusters identified general themes to be pursued, along with some underlying detail. Without ado, the final seven themes were put on to posters around the room and people were asked to physically move to those themes for which they had some enthusiasm. Thus, each theme gathered named action groups. Each group chose their convenor, who set a date for a first group meeting. Within 3 hours, we had moved from a concerned but fragmented assembly, to getting ourselves organised into seven groups around developmental themes ready to get down to business. The real work could then begin.

A GLOBAL BUSINESS ALIGNS TO ITS FUTURE

An international organisation needed to bring people into alignment (as they came from all around the globe, many had never previously met). We designed a 3-day program to surface issues, to bring people into relationship, and having developed a creative frame of mind, to design what future success would look like. The red thread of the program was the thinking process using LVT to enable everyone's ideas to contribute to a shared outcome. Other elements of the program: sunrise seminars, outdoor exercises, theatrical games, collage, and so on, encouraged people to relate in ways that would bring their creativity to bear. For this residential event, the client chose a hotel in Belgium, which had some nice scenery and provided all creature comforts without too many distractions for the 90 attendees.

That red thread comprised a series of sessions:

1. Gather and organise in small groups
2. Cross-present and integrate the diverse outputs
3. Epitomise, make a ring composition, and tell the story of the vision
4. Based on the ring, develop strategies to realise the vision

Initially, groups of five worked independently before merging their outputs as larger subgroups, and eventually, aided by technology (software capture and projection of physical modelling) they worked as a single group on ring composition. Composing the ring and telling the story of the vision was cathartic. Having thus established a believable future together, working on strategies, and committing to action over the coming months were relatively easy. Outputs were immediately posted to the intranet for future reference.

FROM VISION TO STRATEGY

When we have developed a vision of the future, we are faced with the question, 'Now what? How do we make our vision a reality?' Given the right approach, there is every reason to expect that a team will have an audacious view of what can be achieved – far more audacious than adding a few percent to last year's numbers and calling it the plan for the future. **With vision, we start from the future and work backward.** With the right frame of mind, the right circumstances and the right process, a group can be very creative in designing the future it thinks itself worthy of. With the end in mind, designing the way to it from the current position will be relatively straightforward. Significantly, the vision shifts people's mindset. What would be daunting viewed from the past, looks achievable viewed from the future!

Whether you have opted to develop a systems diagram or gone for a ring composition, you will be challenged not to fall back on old patterns. You will need to grasp the novelty of your output and think about what strategies the system demands, if it is to be realised.

If you have developed a ring composition, it should have pushed your thinking to a higher logical level and created new possibilities. As described in Chapter 5, you can take the rungs as representing facets of strategy. In each case, you are challenged to reconcile the opposite ends of the rung – the outward and return journeys – by writing an epitome. Then you can reverse Ishikawa's famous fishbone diagram to plot the transitional steps of your transformational process that arrives at your ideal future from your current reality. Again, we are working back from the future! The main benefit of this exercise is that it shifts minds and reframes issues. Those who participate will be more strategic. As you go forward, you will need to help people not to revert to old mindsets, so that they maintain their creative edge.

VALUES

From the high ground that we achieve within the context of our common purpose (our WHY) and a clear vision (our WHAT) we are able to pause and ask the question, 'Given our intent, what values will we adopt in seeking to achieve it?' Now we address our HOW, considering values from the direction of our intention.

Naturally we all value our values, so we can easily feel personally threatened when there is a need to change them. Yet change will very likely be needed, if we are to align – and then we will have the task of living up to our new values. Many people have experienced an awakening of values in the COVID-19 pandemic, making it possible and necessary to look again at vision and even to reconsider our purpose.

VALUES FILTER INCOMING INFORMATION

In long-standing groups, the values may be no more than implied. Making them explicit will remove much misunderstanding, frustration, and stress. What we value gets noticed and gets attention. We all too easily tune-out information that our values do not recognise, but which may be very significant to the greater whole. That is the clue to 'reprogramming' people's attention to enable them to contribute. Jan Carlzon, in his readable little book, 'Moments of Truth,' chronicles many incidents in which, through Scandinavian Airlines' clear message that individual customers really matter, people in the company felt empowered to act. Carlzon demonstrated that customer focus was not merely a slogan, but a value to be embraced. This enabled him to set aside rules, giving people at all levels full freedom and responsibility for achieving results. Customers experienced the difference in those moments of truth. By showing he really meant what he said, Carlzon turned the airline around!

Here is a way to agree a set of values. Set up good conditions – a safe environment and one not overburdened with messages about past corporate values – the company training room or a boardroom with all its symbolism and pictures of the founding fathers, is unlikely to be conducive to exploration. Take people off-site into convivial surroundings and get them comfortable and relaxed. Bring people into relationship with an interactive exercise and then ask them to talk about themselves in response to value-laden questions. As you model reflective responses, people will begin to experience and to express their own values.

Discussing values can start by taking a look at a hierarchy of values. Peter Vail, of George Washington University, puts forward the following picture. Any organisation exists in a context. Apart from its products or services, it has to relate to a wider community. Internally, it is some sort of home to its employees. The interface between its inner and outer world has two-way traffic to do with the efficacy of its output and its economic viability. In the end, it wants to mean something to its stakeholders, to the world at large, and maybe even to history.

Start by working solo, guided by questions, and then comparing notes in pairs. Interrogate the purpose. Try to identify the stated values in the organisation and any areas of difference between stated values and those reflected in behaviour. Also, identify any differences between personal

Economic	How we prioritise expenditure What gets spent on what?
Technical	Our efficacy How do we do what we do?
Communal	The kind of organisation we want to be What do we want our employees to feel about us?
Socio-Political	The organisation's role in the wider community What do we want people to think about us?
Transcendental	What the organisation wants to mean How do we want history to remember us?

DIAGRAM 7.1
A values hierarchy

and corporate values. This should enable a useful discussion to ensue, from which a list of value statements can be derived.

Get people to plot their values on this model and to further question any areas that seem weak. Often more attention will be given to 'bottom-line' values and less to transformational values. Try to redress the balance by probing deeper – everyone has a need to find meaning and significance in what they do. Expressing that need will help ensure it is not overlooked. Even the humblest person in the organisation can recognise (and be recognised for) the relevance of their contribution to the whole.

One way we have done this is to have people in small groups generate and discuss a list of value words, with the task of selecting the five they consider most important in the organisational context.

An alternative way into discussing values is to have sets of cards with values written on them. In small groups, ask people to select five they think should be core values for the organization. These can be displayed on flipchart or put on to sticky notes or MagNotes so that a composite picture can be developed in plenary session. This will enable the differences between groups to be discussed, in order to arrive at agreed values. In a way, the discussions will be more important than the output. Five core values, that people have explicitly selected, will be a great guide to behaviour.

In this chapter, we have looked at how our leadership develops shared visions, within the context of meaning provided by our common sense of purpose. We have agreed the values we will espouse as we work to realise our visions. In the next chapter, we explore the higher level of abstraction that is to do with purpose.

EXERCISE 7.1: DEVELOP YOUR POWER
OF VISION: STEP ONE

Using sticky notes or similar medium, use your imagination to describe what success looks like.

Conven a group of people who share a purpose and start with a question such as:

> *Imagine it is the year xxxx* (about 5 years from the present) *and that we have achieved all we hoped for.* **What does success look like?** *What do we see going on that is evidence that our ideas worked out well?*

Work independently on the initial gathering of ideas, then pool your ideas to make sure you understand what everyone has said. Make clusters (not categories) of ideas that are mutually relevant. Start with pairs of ideas and then build clusters of no more than six or seven ideas. Let everyone participate, sharing their rationale.

Now write an epitome for each cluster. An epitome is much more than a title. It integrates the whole meaning of the contents, so that it is able to stand for all the detail. It is a summing up, not a simplification. The epitome must be a full statement with a verb and ideally with a subject (often 'we'). Use active language to convey the energy in your epitomes.

Now you can copy your epitomes on to new notes and explore their relationships. What comes before what? What causes what? Are there feedback loops? Reveal the structural relationships that exist so that you begin to understand your vision as a system.

EXERCISE 7.2: DEVELOP YOUR POWER
OF VISION: STEP TWO

As an advanced technique, you might try Ring Composition. This mysterious technique can produce startling insights, so do not despair if your early efforts are not fruitful. Try again.

String your epitomes together to tell a story. Crucially your story should end where it started to form a ring. Experiment with alternative sequences. If you are doing it with others, take turns to try to improve the story. When it hangs together well, test the structure of the ring. Is there correspondence between the outer journey and the return? Will adjustments make it hang together better?

Once you have a good ring composition, take each rung in turn. Now, explore strategies using a fishbone diagram. The two ends of the rung are mutually relevant and you should write a new epitome that resolves the tension between the two, which will be the ideal future.

Draw the spine of the fishbone with the current reality at the left and the desired future on the right. In order to realise your desired future, what primary causes will bring about transformation? Select 3 or 4 main causal threads and assign each to a branch on that line (a fishbone). Identify transitional steps on each branch – milestones on the road towards the end state. See diagram 5.3

Complete your diagram so that you have a map of all the transitions that will culminate in the overall transformation from current reality to desired future.

8

A Sense of Purpose

Making a Meaning-Field

WHY DO WE NEED A SENSE OF PURPOSE?

As we saw when we looked at worlds of perception, purpose and values are at high levels of abstraction – and yet they profoundly influence our daily lives. If we are not clear about our purpose and values, we are likely to experience conflicts and confusions that will dissipate our energies.

People mature individually, most usually when they discover, invent, or subscribe to some cause beyond themselves (they embark on their hero's journey). As they become inwardly integrated, their sense of purpose gives meaning to all they are engaged in. If people share a sense of purpose with others, it gives a shared identity and aligns them all in shared intent, as a living community of interest. Thus, they begin to operate as a unified (whole) system, individually embraced as voluntary sub-systems within it, which gives them meaning and significance.

Such unity will not come about by accident (although a catastrophe might bring it into being). Most of us will need explicit processes to help bring about a collaborative state. Individuals need to feel an increased necessity (a call) to find their inner self, to take charge of their lives, and embark on a developmental path. This can only be voluntary. Manipulation will be ineffective. Compulsion or coercion will be counterproductive.

Until we clarify our individual purpose, we will go hither and thither, propelled by our appetites, seduced by media, or at a loss of where to aim.

Many of us are deeper into this particular mire than we would like to admit. Collectively, it is likely to be even more difficult. We may be caught up in a group or an organisation, doing what is expected, but not in charge of our own destiny. Unless or until we clarify our collective purpose, we are very likely to have different assumptions and be unwittingly pulling in different directions.

Mountaineering may seem to the outsider to be pointless activity. Unless you are exploring, surveying, or film-making, there may well be no tangible outcome from venturing into the mountains, with all its accompanying discomfort and danger. My own personal experience indicates otherwise. Long ago, I discovered that it was always worth the effort of heading out, whatever the weather. At some point, nature would bestow a gift – a beautiful glimpse of distant landscape through a hole in the clouds, the unexpected appearance of a wild creature, or the deep inner satisfaction of difficulty overcome and composure recovered. Often, the worse the conditions, the greater the fulfillment. Insofar as mountaineering has a purpose, it is mostly to be found in discovering your inner self. Perhaps not, as George Mallory famously said of why he wanted to climb Everest, 'Because it is there' but rather its reflection, 'Because I am here?'

REAL OR COUNTERFEIT?

Articulating your common purpose, for it be of value, must be the result of genuine introspection and thinking – a process of exploration. In the corporate world, all too often 'mission statements' are produced superficially – even delegated as a kind of window-dressing operation, done by marketers without soul-searching or due diligence, then consigned to the office wall or used to adorn the annual report. They may impress, but will have little long-term benefit. On the other hand, developing your own statement of purpose will evoke the loftiest, most abstract, value-laden intent. In addition, it will mobilise latent human energies towards realising challenging long-term goals, investing all endeavour with meaning. Furthermore, those who laboured on the task are likely to have shifted their perceptions to the point where they begin to inhabit a different reality.

For example, in our venture at High Trenhouse, we periodically involve all members of staff in articulating our purpose. In general terms, we aim to look after our clients with warm hospitality, making them as welcome and comfortable as is appropriate. We do so with warmth and care, for them and for one another, providing ideal conditions for co-creative work, so that they are helped in achieving their ends. We aim to help them achieve all they aspire to. Their ends become our ends, which means we routinely go well beyond the norms of the hospitality industry. It is in encouraging our team to articulate what we do in their own words, and modelling behaviour, that our purpose as business owners becomes the purpose of our whole team.

A PROCESS OF PURPOSING

The purpose of purposing is to create a field of meaning in which the game is to be played. The 'meaning-field' that is established by a sense of common purpose, empowers each person to find their own role by focusing their personal intent, capacity, and calling. Within that field, as we saw in the last chapter, patterns of possibility, referred to as 'Visions,' illuminate opportunities and guide actions in local areas. Shared visions and values tell every individual how to act, even when there is no overt communication, supervision, or control. To be in the meaning-field is to be *in communication*.

Meaningful purpose bestows unity on a team, community, or organisation. Purpose, insofar as people have been able to commit themselves, defines what is meaningful for them – their beliefs and values, their attitudes, assumptions, and strategies – ultimately their behaviours. Provided the high-level work has been well done, shared meaning will ensure everyone's actions are collectively effective.

Beware! we habitually see reality upside down. A purpose can be more real than what we normally refer to as the real world! What is concrete may appear to have most substance, but it is the most abstract, our beliefs for example, that shape the world within which we act. An authentic statement of purpose will have the effect of clearly focusing personal and collective intent.

So, let us walk through the process. Before setting about brainstorming, take care to articulate a question that is wide-open and generic. The general gist of it needs to be 'Think about the fundamental nature of our endeavour – what is the value we bring to society? **Why** are we doing it?' Beware of being too specific as, for instance, 'What is our purpose in running top-class hotels' Push yourself to a higher level of abstraction. It may well transpire that a more generic question will open up a totally new way of understanding, unlimiting the way people see what they are engaged in. A classic example of this is the breakthrough that Union Pacific experienced when they stopped thinking of themselves as running trains and began to see they were in the business of facilitating mobility. Readers' Digest reframed their business from being a magazine publisher to being in the business of direct mail selling. The more abstract your articulation of purpose, the more freedom you have in realising it.

When you wish to clarify a collective purpose, for family, groups, or organisations, it is worth a little practice with bringing clarity to your own personal purpose. The exercise at the end of this chapter gives you a way to approach this. Do allow enough time – not merely one session but a period of reflecting daily before sitting down to do the exercise – let your mind explore its inner secrets and be prepared for some struggle and some surprises.

TIME AND PLACE

Clarity of purpose is absolutely fundamental to meaningful life or work – and the process should not be hurried. It is worth taking care to create ideal conditions to think about it – to work in pleasant surroundings where you will not be distracted. Remember that in times of crisis, great leaders have traditionally 'gone up into the mountains' to deliberately seek out conditions that enable them to reflect deeply, to think new thoughts, to refresh the soul, the heart, and the mind, so as to return with new insights. For a group, spending (at least) two nights together allows time for relationships to deepen and the process to fully run its course. People should arrange their affairs to make it unnecessary to be disturbed by external matters. Getting away from familiar premises and into neutral territory helps free you from cultural conditioning. If the surroundings are themselves liberating, natural, and inspiring, so much the better. Do not be tempted to introduce irrelevant entertainments, as often happens with corporate groups. It is unlikely to contribute and would be better at some other time. Similarly, adding a 'business agenda' will compromise the real reason for being away. You need a dedicated facility and dedicated time with no distractions and no temptations.

FACILITATORS – INTERNAL OR EXTERNAL

Given the importance of the process of purposing, it needs to be in the right hands. Whereas internals will have the advantage of knowing the organisation and the personalities involved, externals will be free from cultural conditioning and fear of career-limiting gaffs. There are people who have a gift for challenging the status quo, for lifting the spirit, and for enabling teams to surprise themselves. Find them!

WHOSE PURPOSE?

Before beginning the process, it is important to ensure you have gathered the right people in the right circumstances with the right intentions. Consider who needs to own the purpose. If it is a whole organisation, then the most senior people must be involved – and perhaps shareholders, employees, and customers too. Within the overall purpose will be subpurposes involving subsets of owners, and these may need their own independent process. For a community, you need the prime movers and shakers, as well as inviting anyone with enough interest to attend. Take care not to inadvertently alienate any less-than-popular individuals. Cynics have value! The whole system needs to be involved.

Your process has actually begun from the moment you decide to embark on it, so who you invite and how you invite them, begins to shape the event itself. Prepare the psychological ground for creative thinking by making it clear that, through this process, people will be shaping their collective future.

DESIGN

Your event will need to be well-structured in order to bring minds together and to facilitate genuine enquiry. Think of it as a play in three acts: Act One brings people together in relationship, introduces the overall theme, and sets the scene; Act Two engages people in opening up all possibilities – this is the time for divergent thinking in creative space; Act Three looks towards completion of the process and safe landing at the successful outcome. People will return to ordinary life with a job well-done, clarity about how the purpose will inform their own future, and confident that progress will be made.

This is a brief voyage into more abstract worlds, 'itself a cyclic hero's journey.' Start with a warm welcome and create an atmosphere of attentiveness and openness. Some pattern-breaking activity early in the process will be helpful. Playful interactive exercises can surface and overcome hidden assumptions and interpersonal blocks. Later in the process, a reflective excursion in beautiful surroundings can help awaken intuition and inspire higher perceptions. Such elements should be seamlessly integrated into the process, as one whole. All these diverse elements will be held together by the red thread of a thinking process designed to articulate the purpose, feeding in turn into strategies and plans.

CLARIFYING PURPOSE

So how do we find our purpose? For a start, we can think of the purpose of any action, from the most trivial to the hugely important and significant, in terms of the framework:

It is important to differentiate these three, because conflation causes confusion

Our common purpose is:

To:	**WHAT** it is we do that adds value—our functional task
In a way that:	**HOW** we do things—our values and principles
So that:	**WHY** we do what we do—what is it all for? How we fit in the wider context

DIAGRAM 8.1
Purpose framework

This is, of course, a version of the triad we came across in Chapter 2. So, for instance, right now my operational work (**To:**) is in giving form to a set of ideas (yours in reading and reflecting). My leadership work (**In a way that:**) is in grasping the opportunity to share insights with you (yours in entertaining these ideas and checking your own experience to see if they make sense). My strategic work (**So that:**) is in packaging my experience so that it can be helpful to you and your enterprise (your strategic work is positioning my input in the complex of ideas that come your way so that one day you can use it). 'So that' gives us the reason Why – it gives meaning to our efforts and focuses everyone's leadership.

The framework forces us to differentiate our What, How, and Why, which are easily and habitually conflated (i.e., obfuscating rather than clarifying). Making the distinctions is hard work, but very rewarding. This framework, which I learned from Charlie Krone, has proved useful to countless groups, including senior teams in major undertakings, because it helps people understand (and thus, get a grip on) their role, with increased awareness. Making this triad conscious, with the help of a facilitator, will be time very well spent. Because it helps avoid confusions that dissipate energies, it leads to effective action.

A WORKED EXAMPLE

Let me walk you through a typical purposing workshop. In this example, we were asked to help the senior team of a data handling organisation (a dozen people) to clarify their vision – it was only later that we discovered they needed to also clarify their purpose. We designed an off-site residential workshop that would increase awareness, improve relationships, and raise the level of thinking. Some preparatory exercises were undertaken before the event, to encourage participants to question the status quo and tap into their creativity (we all fall into habits of mind and we need to break free from them if we are to invent a new future).

The off-site took place at High Trenhouse – a dedicated residential centre in beautiful surroundings, of which they had exclusive use. After a warm welcome, they were involved in a short exercise that signalled this was not 'business as usual' and that they were themselves the raw material for creative work.

There followed a theme talk – something of the content of this book (not business speak) to nudge them towards a change of perspective. After a convivial meal, a quick collage exercise encouraged them to embrace visual metaphors and surface emotional issues in their current reality – to voice what was usually not spoken about.

Next day started with a sunrise seminar. This pre-breakfast session provided a chance not to 'put on yesterday's habits.' Relaxation, visualisation, and related techniques provoked exploration of people's own thoughts and also raised awareness.

We introduced LVT – thinking with multiple intelligences – 'algebra of the mind' – using magnetic hexagons on portable whiteboards. The planned focus was on developing visions with the trigger question *'It IS (5 years into the future) – What does success look like?'* While working in small groups, everyone became totally absorbed in pooling their ideas and good outcomes were achieved. Because the process is intensive and demanding, we extended the lunch break with an outdoor session. This brought people's bodies into play – actual physical engagement to help balance cerebral overload. The primary aim was to help people practice the arts of both giving and receiving feedback, upon which all learning depends.

Although the Vision work went very well, including ring composition, it became apparent that, because this venture involved a major change of direction, the group was not sufficiently clear about its purpose. A shift of thinking was needed!

In a crisis meeting with the project owner, we proposed to deal with this issue immediately, without dispersing and having to reconvene the group on a later occasion. Because people were gathered and in a prepared state to be able to work intensively, we could compress the process. The program was rapidly revised in order that purpose could be addressed on the last day.

The next sunrise seminar used a reading exercise, developed from Idries Shah's materials. In turn, people chose a book at random, read a random passage, and then interpreted how that passage informed the work of the group. The challenge of random association obliged people to draw upon their inner wisdom to illuminate the group's raison d'etre, thereby changing the level of interaction.

To start the purpose session, we looked briefly at who had a stake in the business. Then, once more using LVT and working in subgroups, in half an hour we gathered ideas on 'what is our common purpose?'

The subgroups structured their output using the **To: In a way that; So that** framework, and then cross-presented. Next, they merged the different inputs on to three boards, one for each term of the triad, manned in rotation by representatives from each subgroup, so that everyone was engaged. The material on each board was clustered and epitome titles composed. Quite quickly, the whole thing was brought together and then read out loud, so everyone had buy-in to the final version. A core mission was quickly singled out (the core is the 'so that' – the ultimate Why – which will be articulated differently for each group of stakeholders) and a purpose statement carefully composed.

With purpose clarified they were able, again in parallel groups, to set out 'Next Steps' for the months ahead and we closed the workshop on time, having added an unexpected layer of value to the process. Normally you would clarify purpose before vision, because that would ensure you were aligned. In this case, we inadvertently got it back to front – but through dint of focus, hard work and good fortune, it worked well.

In this chapter, we have looked at a specific process for exploring and articulating a sense of purpose – hugely important, because it creates a meaning-field for everyone's endeavours. You might ponder on how the process just described maps on to the hero's journey or the enneagram. Where does it deviate from either cyclic pattern? Do you see why we employed such devices as collage, exercises, readings and sunrise seminars?

In the next chapter, we will consider the decision required to take us into the realm of action. How do we find the commitment that will meet the challenge?

EXERCISE 8: DEVELOP A SENSE OF PURPOSE

This is an introductory personal exercise to help you get familiar with the topic and think about your own purposes at this time of your life. What seems to be significant to you and what, if anything, do you feel is missing? Give yourself time and space for the exercise – Enjoy a day in surroundings where you feel relaxed and happy.

Equip yourself with cards or sticky notes. Write down every aspect of your purpose that comes to you. Start with an intensive burst and then gather more material through the day as you allow yourself to relax and reflect. Toward the end of the day, be sure to be undisturbed as you make a display in which you separate '**To**,' '**In a way that**,' and '**So that**.' Now you can cluster and write epitomes. It might be good to reflect on your results so far, before you articulate your personal sense of purpose.

You could usefully repeat this exercise periodically – perhaps, each year on your birthday? Apart from anything else it will give you a better grasp of the nature of purpose as well as giving direction to your life.

9

Commitment

Embark on Your Hero's Journey

COMMITMENT AS AN ACT OF WILL

When we are ready, we can act. That requires a decision – an act of will that commits us to the endeavour. Of course, commitment does not guarantee success – we sometimes commit to a venture that eventually fails – but commitment calls forth our very best, even at the risk of loss, injury, or death. When we are committed, it is as if we are naked before God. Our commitment moves our starting point – indeed, it changes the world.

Jim Rohn, the motivational speaker, liked to illustrate the principle with the story of Gideon from the Old Testament. Gideon, a simple farmer, was called by God to help his tribe fight the Midianites (Judges 6,7). Gideon gathered 30,000 men (the Midianites had 300,000). Even so, God told him he had too many and he should allow those who wished to leave to return home. 27,000 quit, but God still said there were too many. He told Gideon to have the men march up and down in the hot sun then give them a break on the riverbank. Those who lapped the water like dogs, spear in hand were to be retained, and the rest dismissed. That left Gideon with 300. But these men were totally committed! With this small band of intrepid warriors, he defeated his enemies!

WHAT IS THIS QUALITY OF COMMITMENT?

Finding oneself 'naked before God' is scary. It implies being faced with a significant challenge, with nobody but you to deal with whatever unexpectedness or terror occurs. It further implies something has brought you to a state where all other concerns are set aside and you have no baggage. Now only your decisiveness can resolve the situation – and the outcome is by no means certain!

We can have many so-called 'good intentions' but true commitment significantly changes our relationship with reality, fundamentally shifting our starting point. Only you can provide the 'act of will' in your world! In your state of metaphorical nakedness, can you find it in yourself to respond with a categorical 'Yes?' To be able to do so, you will need to prepare yourself for such a momentous occasion. Prepare to seize the day!

High Trenhouse, our centre on Malham Moor, is at 1300 ft above sea level. Being close to the watershed between the North and Irish Seas, it gets the brunt of winter storms whichever direction they come from. We expect winter challenges, so when the roads get blown-in with snow we are not fazed. We know that if conditions permit, snow ploughs will come through by late afternoon and we may need to seize the short window of opportunity before the roads are blown-in again. This usually provides a chance to get staff or clients in or out and to get supplies. It can be challenging and yet only twice in 40 years have we had people snowed in – and they experienced it as a huge bonus! However, we had one group organiser who thought we exaggerated the risk and declined our suggestion that we should move cars to the valley. As conditions deteriorated, he changed his mind, but it was too late. We tried leading a convoy to the valley but one by one, all the cars got stuck. We managed a retreat, leaving only one car abandoned. The next day, when a different attitude prevailed, we hit the window and managed to get vehicles down to the main road. The abandoned car remained stuck for 2 weeks!

We often dither when we could be decisive but to be decisive requires that 'act of will.' Most of us get along by fudging this issue. We pretend to decide – we go through the motions, but our decision is weak because we have not learned the power of commitment. There can be no pretence! There will be only you, wholeheartedly doing what you have undertaken, with no guarantee of success. You stand alone, four-square in front of your challenge. You will certainly get a result, but it may not be what you expected. It is therefore imperative that you learn what you can from the experience, through objective observation and reflection.

ONLY YOU!

On one of those occasions when I was in the Alps on my own, I found a reasonably competent climbing partner with whom to climb the steep north face of the Grepon. This necessitated staying overnight in a tiny hut, strapped to a miniscule ledge on the mountain. Unfortunately, bad weather the next day obliged us to stay a second night for which we had not brought provisions. The following day we were eager to do our route and descend on other side, down to the valley. We led alternately but my companion was overly desperate and began to take risks. Eventually he lost his grip and slid down a slab of rough granite, lacerating his finger-tips. If we were not to withdraw, I had to rise to the challenge and lead the remainder of the route. Where I had been diffident, I now had to be strong. I was delighted to discover that commitment gave me enough courage to successfully tackle the dramatic airy crux that brought us on to the top of the mountain.

There is a trap for the unwary. It is quite possible, in our strange society, to gain all the badges of achievement by being embedded in groups or organisations that carry you along. You can have the trappings of success without ever actually earning them. In that case to be naked before God will turn into a terrifying experience, because you are not properly prepared. If you are used to support from subordinates; if you have gotten your results because you have access to levers of power; if you are a successful manipulator; if you are used to charming your way through difficult situations; then to be alone will be rather frightening and may cause you to disfunction. Hence, it is good to practise before you meet your ultimate challenge, which may just be your last battle on earth.

Prepare for your hero's journey. Work on presence, patience, thoughtfulness, courage, creativity, love. These qualities grow as we practise them. Although they may bring no direct result, the accumulation of virtues gives us access to extraordinary capabilities.

EVOKE THE POWER OF WILL

The committed self is a power to be reckoned with. From a state of empti-ness one can call forth one's deeper self, through commitment. Doubt, weakness, lack of confidence, indecision are your adversaries which may prevent such an outcome. Arrogance or pretence will not cut it. Only your authentic self will do. Hence all the work you put in to discover, train, exercise, and strengthen that authenticity, will bear fruit at the criti-cal moment. Athletes and performers know this well, as they dedicate themselves to such preparation. We can choose to live impeccably. In our everyday routines, in our daily dealings, and in our undertakings, we can promise ourselves to be true to our principles, to be upstanding, to be trustworthy, to be strong.

Commitment is not emotional – it is not an affair of the heart, nor even of the head. It is a decision of great moment, because it is an 'act of will.' It is a decision whose outcomes will have consequences, particularly for your own soul. That does not mean that you will necessarily be willing to die in the attempt to fulfill what you have decided upon – but you will not let go lightly. If you do have to concede defeat, you will do so with humility and in a way that ensures you learn from the experience, in order that you may try again another day. It is a hero's journey in miniature.

> Until one is committed there is the chance to draw back; always ineffective-ness. Concerning all acts of initiative (and creation) there is one elementary truth, the ignorance of which kills countless ideas and splendid plans: that the moment one definitely commits oneself, then providence moves too.
>
> All sorts of things occur to help one that would not otherwise have occurred. A whole stream of events issues from the decision, raising in one's favour all manner of unforeseen incidents and meetings and material assistance which no man would have dreamed would come his way.
>
> **W. H. Murray**
> *Leader, Scottish Mountaineering Club*
> *Himalayan Expedition 1951*

Every performer knows that, however well you prepare, there is no know-ing what will happen when you enter the fray. All you can control is your own state. Other players bring unknowable influences. The outcome is an emergent quality of the interaction. It is like that, for instance, when you run an organisational or community event. It is like that when you have some audacious plan to act in the real world or to change it. Unless there is uncertainty it cannot be a truly creative action. You welcome that uncertainty as your teacher and you accept the lessons your results provide.

As described in Chapter 7, we were once contracted to help a senior team articulate their vision and only when we had this well in hand did it become apparent that they had no shared sense of purpose. There was a danger they would fragment in their strategies and actions. Although time was short, we agreed to abandon the planned programme so as to make sure a clear sense of purpose was hammered out, so that they could return to vision with a single mind. Making the necessary demands on people's attention and energies was very exacting work – a challenge to the facilitator's commitment. In spite of the additional challenge, it was a very successful workshop. People left the event with both purpose and vision defined and with shared strategies for achieving their desired outcomes.

Commitment communicates! However, it should not be coercive. It does not achieve outcomes by exerting power. Instead, commitment communicates confidence, strength, assurance, and trust. It is a great enabler. More than that, as Murray says, providence moves too. Whatever providence may be, it is a valuable resource to summon to your aid in your hour of need.

EXERCISE 9.1: WILL

Will is a deep fundamental power – like a power loaned by God – not to be confused with mere 'will-power' or determination. Will is the capacity to bring intention into your affairs. In others, we see the manifestation of 'will' as strength. Its absence leads to weakness, resulting in a life of disappointment and frustration – ultimately to a lack of any personal power. This capacity can (and must) be developed.

Nothing gets achieved without commitment, but we may lack the strength to commit to major objectives, and thus, be discouraged by our own incapacity. We can increase that capacity through practice. For that we should start with little things. The following very simple, yet potent, exercise is recommended, as a way to explore and develop 'will' in your own life. It is an exercise to return to periodically (perhaps when you become aware of drifting or losing contact) as a means of gaining strength and achieving more control of your life and work. The exercise needs to be distinguished from ordinary behaviour (do not use it to tackle your to-do list!) and to be done with absolute rigour. There is no point in cheating on such an important, life-governing faculty.

It is a good idea to do the exercise for a period of 1 or 2 weeks and then give it a break. For that period, set yourself to give it your absolute best. Do not tolerate failure or you are colluding in your own downfall. Contract with yourself to pay a penalty if things go wrong – to get up extra early, to take a cold bath, to give money to charity, etc. – whatever works for you as a real penalty – on each and every occasion that you fail in your selected task. Increase the penalties for persistent failure. Now to the exercise itself!

EXERCISE 9.2: WILL – DECISION EXERCISE

You need to select a simple task that is **not dependent on the actions of others**, though it might involve other people. To begin with, tasks can be very simple indeed – to move an object, tidy your desk, send a letter, use a particular greeting, smile at someone, etc. Later, you can be more ambitious and use the exercise in relation to bigger tasks but avoid using the exercise to tackle your to-do list (incidentally, tasks that hang around become invisible burdens and actually sap your 'will').

Having chosen a small task for tomorrow, just before you go to sleep, rehearse the task in as much detail as your imagination can provide – actually see yourself doing the task, sense the movements of your limbs, hear the sounds, and smell the smells – see the task getting done, step-by-step, until you see the final result and you know it is done. Having thus rehearsed, ask yourself whether you really intend to do it. Take care not to decide to act unless you are confident in your success (and know the penalty of failure). Next day as you waken, remember your decision. During the day you perform the task, ideally with some awareness of your preparation the night before. **That's it!**

Reflect upon and note the outcome, especially as you prepare a new task for the next day. If you forget, undergo the penalty and resolve not to forget again. Of course, the easiest thing is to forget to prepare, so view preparation as part of the task and penalise yourself for lack of preparation. Do not do the task unless you have prepared, otherwise you are merely doing chores, not doing this exercise!

There are, thus, the following steps:

1. Pick a suitable task
2. Mentally rehearse before you go to sleep.
3. Decide to act
4. Remember your decision in the morning
5. Do the task
6. At the end of the day, reflect on the result
7. Take the penalty, if you fail

Be consistent and systematic and do not try to kid yourself – to do so is pointless and counterproductive. Note whether you perceive any effects in your life.

Give yourself a break after a week or so and return to it periodically when you feel the need.

10

The Author's Own Journey

A PATTERN FOR LIVING

To help you understand the structure and stages of the hero's journey to maturity – especially, of course, how it might apply in your own life – I will briefly share my own story. The titles of the stages refer to the archetypical model, derived from antiquity. One of the first and perhaps the most famous hero's journey is Homer's story of Odysseus. He, you may recall, went off to fight for Helen of Troy, somewhere around 800 BC. After struggling against all odds, he returned home 20 years later to bring his story to a violent conclusion. In the introduction to the Penguin edition of the book, translator E. V. Rieu points out that the story is not told in linear temporal sequence. If we were to read the enneagram as a linear sequence, we would have:

1. In the world but not of it
2. Respond to the call
3. Cross the threshold
4. Learn to learn – growth through trials
5. Into the melting pot
6. Naked before God
7. The self awakes
8. Gift of deeper knowledge
9. Integrate to wholeness
10. Return home

Apart from being rather pedestrian (no flashbacks, no parallel plots) such a structure would not have told the story *as a whole*.

In telling my own story, we look instead, firstly at the triad (stages 0, 3, 6) which gives us the whole purpose and substance of the hero's journey – i.e.

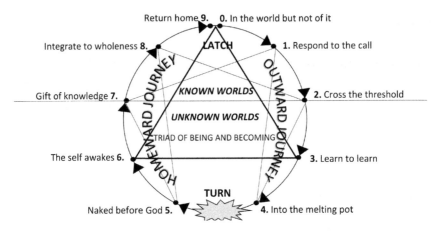

DIAGRAM 10.1
The hero's journey

the transformation of the hero's being. Only then do we follow the inner pattern of the enneagram, visiting stages 1, 4, 2, 8, 5, 7 to discover the process that brought it about. In conclusion we arrive 'home again' at stage 9.

THE TRIAD OF DEVELOPMENT (POINTS 0, 3, 6)

In my youth, I had no knowledge of function, being and will (alternative words for skill, capacity and intent) interacting as a triad – indeed I had never heard of a triad until I met J. G. Bennett! However, only the interaction between these three impulses, as they matured in me, has given me the capability to work with senior managers, helping them clarify their intent, to think effectively together and to individually and collectively make steps in their development and relationships

Looking back, I can see how the action of this triad led to my decision to set up High Trenhouse as a learning centre and to learn through engaging with the work itself. That consisted, initially, of survival, sustainability and reciprocal maintenance with youngsters as clients. Later there followed interactive work that developed managers and others. Looking further back, I see the roots of the idea in design thinking and my architectural practice, my adventures in mountaineering and my personal search for meaning. Through the latter I found my first teacher and guide, J. G. Bennett, ultimately sealing my fate by attending his course at Sherborne. Or earlier still, to my exploits as a boy, playing in the woods on the riverbank, making the most of post-war austerity and isolation, wondering what it would be to become a man.

In 1990, we were picking up the pieces at High Trenhouse, after the departure of Gary and his following. Emerging from the wreckage, we re-built, re-furbished and re-positioned ourselves, originally as a management consultancy with meeting facilities and accommodation. Having dabbled on the fringes of consultancy for several years, I now urgently needed to practise the art in order to pay the bills. I encountered, and learned from, some exceptional influencers. I re-connected with Anthony Blake, with whom I had run the International Gurdjieff Society. By 1995 I was well established, learning from every client relationship and from every co-facilitator I brought in. I was privileged to integrate this rich mix of influences into a way of coaching and facilitating which proved highly effective. We divided the specialist venue business from the facilitation practice, setting the latter free to work across the world.

In this process, there matured within me the work I had done in the '80s, as well as all the foundational experience I had had since acquiring High Trenhouse. However, the seeds were surely sown in my formative years, enabling me to find my sense of purpose by drawing upon the idea that life is about becoming whole as a human being. We are each invited to make our hero's journey of discovery, adventuring through those unknown worlds of perception. On the way I came to recognise the triad as a serious phenomenon, one that would illuminate my work with client groups.

The Triad Point 0: Enjoying Normal Life – In the World but Not of It

When I was 8 years old, my parents split. At first, I lived with my father in the family home on the outskirts of York. After school I helped him in his work as a watchmaker. In our long hours together, he laid the seeds of enquiry in my mind. Particularly he implanted the important idea that, to truly become a man, to become one, whole, with full integrity, was no mean ambition.

When I won a scholarship to King James's Grammar School, I left York to join my mother and elder sister living in the countryside. We were poor in those early post-war years, so I acquired simple tastes and an appetite for playing in the wilds, never quite embracing the normal life of my peers. I took to canoeing and, later, to mountaineering, which in those days provided a low-cost medium of adventure. National Service further widened my horizons.

Assigned at one point to a helicopter squadron, I was involved in plucking to safety the crew of the tugboat, Roumania, as she broke up in a storm.

I had become interested in design and, after demob, I studied at Leeds School of Architecture. For a decade I had climbed extensively in the UK and Europe and then a serious Alpine accident, in which I watched two colleagues fall to their deaths down a slope I had just descended, left me somewhat humbled and confused. That same year, 1962, I had joined J. G. Bennett's community at Coombe Springs. Bennett was a polymath, author, scientist, and teacher of Gurdjieffian ideas. His teaching incorporated insights from Islam, Buddhism, Hinduism, Jainism, and so on, long before such ideas became popular in the west. He travelled the world to meet enlightened people and absorb the fundamentals of their knowledge. He learned avidly, in order to transmit to others. A big hearted and hugely energetic man, he was an extraordinary role model.

At Coombe Springs I met Liz and shortly afterwards we married and started a family, moving into a little house nearby, in Kingston upon Thames. We had a loving home and for a decade we enjoyed suburban family bliss. After Coombe, I joined an international design group and eventually established my own architectural practice. I loved that I worked from home and could occasionally pack family and work into the car and drive off to the mountains. Life was a bed of roses.

'Be in the world but not of it' is an admonition I first heard from Idries Shah. It demands you be effective but without identification with worldly concerns. I have tried to practise it but, on the other hand, I have found such detachment in some ways problematic. There were times when worldly passion might have brought me worldly wealth! In a way, 'the world' and I seem, inadvertently, to have been on parallel tracks.

The Triad Point 3: Learn to Learn from Experience

In order to pursue the idea of setting up a learning centre, my wife and I attended Bennett's fourth course at Sherborne in 1974 (the year he died). Afterwards we spent a year searching for property. Eventually, having sold our house, we bought High Trenhouse, arriving there with our two children in 1976. The early days were a struggle. The place was near-derelict and required a huge amount of work on our shoestring budget. Apart from anything else, we needed planning permission and, because we were 'not farmers,' the authorities put every obstacle in our way.

The first winter brought hardship – it was cold and primitive. We made do with a chemical toilet and were briefly reduced to melting snow for drinking water. There were sometimes snowdrifts in our living room and, at one point, we were completely snowbound for 2 weeks. While we had started renovating the property, we began to explore practical learning, with whoever would tolerate the primitive conditions – mostly people on low budgets, falling through society's safety net. With them, we learned a great deal. Aspiring to self-sufficiency, we acquired cows, pigs, and ducks and started a small dairy business. We were greatly helped by people with more maturity than we could muster: friends renting space eased our cash flow while strengthening our resources: an inspirational local farmer would drop by to give valuable advice (possibly out of pity for the cow) without ever appearing to do so; former colleagues and associates brought paying groups and provided practical support to help us along.

As our capability expanded, the focus of our learning became more clearly defined as 'personal and collective development towards wholeness.' Visitors became temporary members of our community and the idea of 'reciprocal maintenance' provided the medium. The process was honed in the early '80s when Anthony Blake and I ran the International Gurdjieff Society from High Trenhouse. By then we had begun to work with a smattering of management groups.

After Bennett's death his followers sought a successor and when they took up with Gary Chicoine, all our lives were disrupted. In 1984, many of us were engaged in a research pilgrimage, under Gary's direction. We travelled in pairs the length and breadth of India, far from the tourist trails and all on a shoestring. We researched, recorded and filmed extraordinary sages and saints of various faiths, wherever we could find living manifestations of India's extraordinary spiritual heritage. It greatly expanded our horizons and tested our resolve.

The Triad Point 6: The Self Awakes

Hard work, sacrifice and determination had brought us to a new quality of being that set the scene for all that was to follow. As the pilgrimage drew to a close, Gary moved to Yorkshire and his uncompromising teaching style put us all under immense pressure. Amongst several relationship shifts, my wife went off with someone else and I was joined by Bernadette, who had been at High Trenhouse in the '70s. With her assistance, I began to integrate all I had learned, in order to redirect it towards developing management groups. At the same time, we invested in upgrading High Trenhouse for the purpose. We gave up being a smallholding because we needed to convert the buildings and grounds. With Janet Mills, I set up a partnership, Leading Edge, in order to practise coaching and facilitation. I was also involved with Hodgson and Heath in various management-related projects. However, circumstances resulted in Gary taking over High Trenhouse, lock, stock, and barrel, to accommodate his family and his following, which completely disrupted our incremental progress.

When, a couple of years later, Gary and Co. left for Scotland, we found ourselves stripped out, in debt, with no business and with a large property in need of total renovation. Although we were tempted to abandon our project for the sake of an easier life, we chose instead to commit to a fresh start: to shoulder the burden of debt, to rebuild, and re-launch our enterprise so as to serve its original purpose. This was an enormous task on all fronts for which we had only our two selves as resource. Nevertheless, that momentous decision was the making of us, leading to an incredibly creative and productive period. There is no mistaking the nature of this stage of the hero's journey!

To begin with, we hoped to be compensated by Gary and his group. When this was not forthcoming, we initiated legal proceedings. However, the lawyers screwed up, which led us to rethink. We scrapped the proceedings and, incredibly, the law firm refunded our money – Wow! Gary was released from threat and we were spared the ignominy of suing our spiritual benefactor. Now we could focus on tackling the real challenge.

It took many months of intense work on all fronts. We went even deeper into debt but managed to convince financial backers, as well as potential customers, that we knew where we were headed. We were learning very fast and made remarkable progress. I travelled frequently to London seeking business, while organisations throughout the country discovered the unique qualities of our dedicated residential centre and developmental facilitation. Now, many years later, the whole project continues to be a demanding commitment, keeping us youthful and focussed.

The Journey Point 1: Respond to the Call

Bennett's eclecticism had brought him into contact with Idries Shah, a Sufi teacher, author and translator of ancient teachings (Shah's Sufi teaching stories are well worth seeking out). In 1965, Bennett persuaded the

Institute to gift Coombe Springs to Shah. (He promptly sold it for housing development!) The Institute later operated from Bennett's home until, in his 70s, he felt compelled to make his knowledge available to a younger generation. To that end, he toured the globe to promote a 5-year cycle of year-long residential courses. He returned to the UK with a hundred students signed up for the first course, but no property in which to do it. At short notice, he acquired a faded stately mansion, Sherborne House in Gloucestershire, where he established his International Academy for Continuous Education.

In this period, during which I was running my own architectural practice, my wife, Liz, and I ran various art workshops and I had taken an interest in national park study centres, which were a new government initiative. I was astonished to discover that the national parks were setting up centres to study conservation and interpretation. In stark contrast, I had thought such centres would be studying the special quality the parks were intended to protect as a resource for the nation: i.e., studies that would bring people into spiritual contact with the living earth and natural beauty. To resolve this conflict, I became possessed by the idea of setting up a centre of my own. The concept was to bring together my experience in mountaineering and architecture, my wife's art and passion for teaching, along with Bennett's philosophy and methods, as a kind of latter-day Bauhaus. It was an audacious idea – a distinct and persistent call!

The Journey Point 4: Into the Melting Pot – When the Pupil Is Ready the Teacher Appears!

The Institute continued to sustain Bennett's work after his untimely death in 1974, while its governing body looked out for someone to replace him as their teacher and guide. The person they found broke all norms and niceties. At first, he was in touch with individuals by personal correspondence, under the pseudonym of Swami Dadaji Narayan. Dadaji later revealed himself as an American named Gary Chicoine, who, in spite of the stark contrast with Bennett's gentlemanly style, won the approval of the Institute's council. In what seemed a logical extension of our exposure to esoteric knowledge, several of us spent short periods with Gary in Montana and were drawn into the voluntary submission of discipleship. Although Bennett was my first teacher and brought me to the threshold, it was Gary who was to thrust me into the melting pot.

In 1987, Gary was established in premises an hours' drive through the hills from High Trenhouse. Bernadette and I visited regularly for group meetings. Quite unexpectedly, we were asked to accommodate the group, ostensibly as a temporary measure in response to a crisis. I believed it a blessing to have my guru come to my home – and in hindsight, it really was. However, our guests swiftly adopted the host position. All accommodation was occupied by Gary, his family, his disciples and their families, as well as a school for the children and various research projects. Very quickly our home and our enterprise were subsumed, providing the total disruption that would transform the scope of our ambitions.

The Journey Point 2: Cross the Threshold

My first wife, Liz, and I, had set ourselves up on this unpredictable adventure when, having had the idea of a learning centre, we abandoned suburban comfort in search of an alternative path. To begin with, we lacked resources and were naïve. Because uprooting was going to change our lives and that of our children, we hesitated, tempted to cling to the comfort and security of suburbia. However, the idea triumphed. Eventually we rented our house to a Japanese rock musician and, to gain relevant experience, we signed up to Bennett's fourth course at Sherborne House. Bennett sadly died the year we were there, but we completed his course.

Still passionate to establish our own centre, we elected not to return to our former home, as we felt that suburban normality would quickly engulf us again. We sold our house and moved to a cottage in Yorkshire, whence we spent a year searching from coast to coast for a suitable property for our venture. In 1976 I bought High Trenhouse at auction (almost by accident through trying to help the auctioneer) and suddenly **we were committed!**

The Journey Point 8: Integrate to Wholeness

After Gary and his entourage left, through the '90s and into the next millennium, Bernadette and I continued to evolve our developmental offering to management, organisations and communities. I was privileged to meet significant trail-blazing pioneers, such as Edward De Bono (lateral thinking), Eli Goldratt (*The Goal* and *Theory of Constraints*), Lou Tice (Pacific

Institute), Charlie Krone (influenced by Bennett), Robert Fritz (Path of Least Resistance) and Valerie Souchkov (TRIZ), as well as many outstanding coaches and facilitators, from whom I learned elements of my craft. In the '80s, trading as Leading Edge, we had worked with first-line managers but now, re-incarnated as Centre for Management Creativity, our offering evolved rapidly to be relevant to ever-more-senior people. Of course! We were successfully integrating diverse fragments into a coherent whole!

As our client groups began to encompass leadership teams of major organisations, we developed both the facilitation and the venue, which became separate businesses. We spun off an outdoor experiential-learning business and developed LogoVisual Thinking, which became the basis of our products business. We worked with community groups and educators, as well as with major national and international organisations throughout the UK and abroad. It was a hugely creative period and very energising. Very many individuals and many organisations continue to benefit.

The Journey Point 5: Naked before God

Gary's sojourn at High Trenhouse certainly acted as a melting pot. Taken over by his entourage, we suspended all aspects of our business and adopted roles within his community. The whole outfit eventually became rather cultish, not helped, I am sure, by my willingness to yield to every provocation. This may well have been a disservice to everyone. On several occasions I was sent off with Bernadette, to look for alternative premises in Scotland, whilst being constantly pushed and cajoled into releasing the last remnant of control of my property.

This brought us to a crisis. I was told I would be dismissed, unless I signed everything over. Whereas I desperately wanted to serve the 'guru,' even deeper down I felt that parting with High Trenhouse would be a betrayal of my mission in life. I was profoundly tormented by the dilemma. Ultimately, finding myself incapable of letting go, I was reduced to utter despair! The upshot was that Bernadette and I were ostracised and the whole outfit went off to Scotland, leaving us with only the physical, emotional and financial wreckage. We took stock! Dare we stay and take on the considerable challenges of starting all over again?

The Journey Point 7: Gift of Deeper Knowledge

Deeper knowledge – or more precisely esoteric knowledge, had been in my background for decades. Right from my father's early pointers, through Fitzgerald's 'Rubaiyat' and Gollancz's anthology, 'From Darkness to Light,' which stimulated further exploration. I eventually studied Gurdjieff with Bennett, Sufism with Idries Shah, and even co-ran IGS (International Gurdjieff Society). Architecture (design thinking) and mountaineering (adventure and commitment) were big influences. I picked up many fragments of knowledge, yet struggled to find relationship between the pieces. Until 1990, that is, when Gary and Co. departed and High Trenhouse became ours once again. From a desperate beginning, that was a year of extraordinary challenge, of total commitment, of hard physical work, of designing, constructing and strategising, as we set out once more to make a learning centre. Now everything made sense. We had a much clearer idea of what was to be learned and by whom. We had acquired hard-earned treasure – practical knowledge and a philosophy of enquiry and meaning-making. With it, we aimed to help make a better world! After toiling on a major refit we were ready to relaunch as The Centre for Management Creativity. Thus, we embarked upon a period of enterprise, deep-learning and co-creation, realised within ourselves.

The Triad Point 9: Return Home – Higher Integration

This is not yet the end of my story, although that can't be very far off. However, we can now see that the triad, described at the outset, has expanded. The function, being and will (or skill, capacity and intent) of that arrogant young architect, who first dreamed of setting up a learning centre, became something more powerful and transformative through pursuit of a purpose.

The journey does not end until it is over – and that comes about when all the parts are integrated into one coherent whole. The self becomes one with the al – or at least you get a little closer to such a possibility. My own journey continues as I seek to communicate something of the nature of learning, so that I can let go. To that end, a little of the essence of my life experience is contained in this book, by way of a developmental psychology. I hope it might help you discover a more holistic view of life and to wonder at life's mystical potential.

Growing Within

I urge you to see how you can apply the knowledge in this book in your daily life. These are disturbing times. Not only climate change, but depletion of resources, economic breakdown and the hubris of powerful yet undeveloped beings, will force humanity into making major adjustments. Perhaps the pause brought about by the COVID-19 pandemic, will be grasped as the opportunity to change direction and build new, more humane and sustainable global systems. That is your challenge! The ideas in this book do not merely inform but can also transform – if you will let them. Through your living, you can change the way humanity organises itself, so that it might evolve a more wholesome society and a more sustainable presence among the earth's multiple life forms. I hope you will pick up the pointers and that they will enable you to progress your own journey to maturity and wholeness, so shining a light for others.

EXERCISE 10: YOUR OWN JOURNEY – A
WORK IN PROGRESS

Using the Hero's Journey as a template, plot your own journey so far. Do so first in linear sequence because that will help you plot the significant events. Take your time, because events need to re-emerge and to re-arrange your memory. You may find that even really important factors have faded as your life has changed course. Try to identify each of the stages of the hero's journey – your own journey! It will help if you make a visual display that you can add to as you remember.

Do this over a period of time – a few weeks perhaps – to allow your recollections to gather on your display and inform one another. Carefully explore periods of confusion or issues of bitterness or disappointment. You will have taken a stance, perhaps, and now, from a distant perspective, you can re-interpret dispassionately. Allow yourself to see emerging patterns and how one part of your life influences all others. With the wisdom of hindsight, you may reach a new understanding of where you are and where you need to go next. Bring yourself to forgive perceived wrongs, let go any bitterness and reconcile any errors.

Later you can try looking at it all through the lens of the enneagram. This will give you a better grasp of the wholeness that you are realising in your life.

Enjoy the process and relish the content. Your life is unique and only you can ensure it is lived rightly. Be at peace and make the most of the time that remains to you. Become fully human.

Epilogue

SO WHAT HAVE WE DISCOVERED?

What does the journey we have taken in this book tell us about leadership as meaning-making or the hero's journey or how to live a good life? It has certainly explored ideas that are not taught in the business schools. After introducing the hero's journey, we looked at the worlds of perception that we, as hero, elect to explore, gathering the experience that will bring us towards maturity and wholeness. We looked at the universal pattern of the enneagram, the hidden pattern of our acts in the real world, which, it appears, is a microcosm of the hero's journey. We paid special attention to the triad of Skill, Capacity, and Intent that manifests the state of our inner development through our acts in the world 'out there,' where it shows up as Operations, Leadership, and Strategy. We followed this by looking at how the patterns of our thinking enable us to make meaning. Especially we considered how the narrative form of Ring Composition may be not merely a story-telling formula, but a reflection of how narratives naturally originate. It suggests that the enneagram is not an invented framework, but a discovery of the natural pattern that makes what is meaningful. When we learn to use Ring Composition, we employ our most subtle perceptions to tune into faint signals we can amplify and realise.

So, when we hear 'the call,' is it not that we simply become aware of the 'urge to meaning,' immanent in nature, in which we can choose to be instrumental? Is finding our hero's journey anything less than our own enactment of the journey to meaning? And when we make that journey, are we not practising leadership as meaning-making – leading the way into unknown worlds, and setting an example for others to follow? Meanwhile, through our work, we can shine a light for all around. Is our living worth anything less than our boldest endeavours?

We looked at leadership and teamwork as natural processes by which people can self-organise and co-create. We explored ways of engaging people in defining a sense of purpose, pushing their thinking to a higher level of abstraction ('algebra of the mind') in pursuit of strategic capability. We explored using Ring Composition to elicit visions and the need to clarify values. Finally, we looked at the role of commitment, in ensuring the realisation of one's efforts and the development of self through decisive action in the world. My own story is added in the hope it might help illuminate some of the principles that will guide your own journey.

Can you see that, as we make our own individual hero's journey, we take meaning-making into our own hands? That the cycles of nature show up as cyclic forms, reflected in our thinking? By tuning into these cycles, we can learn to integrate parts into coherent natural wholes. Is it not possible that by becoming sensitive to wholeness, we humans might just learn to be more wholesome, as individuals, communities and societies, able to self-organise ourselves, in harmony with the rest of life on planet earth? … Perhaps – but the choice is yours! To do nothing is not an option.

Examine where you are within your individual life. Your hero's journey beckons!

Whatever you can do, or dream you can, begin it!

Boldness has genius, power and magic in it.

Goethe, as quoted by W. H. Murray

Bibliography

These are books that I have found useful as sources of inspiration and support in my own journey. Some I regard as friends and would strongly recommend as being worth reading and worth having to hand. In some cases, it is enough to have them available and to be able to use the index. Others one could dip into to find the juicy bits. Some are worth reading cover to cover – and some to read and re-read as food for the mind.

Albrecht, Albert, *Brain Power*, Prentice Hall, 1980.
A book to challenge the way we think we perceive and what is needed to stimulate creativity.

Bateson, Gregory, *Steps to an Ecology of Mind*, Ballantine, 1972.
Every thinking person should have read this book. Valuable insights clearly expounded – one of those authors it is a pleasure to have 'met'.
Other relevant titles: *Mind and Nature, Where Angels Fear to Tread*

Bennett, John G, *The Dramatic Universe*, Coombe Springs Press, 1966.
Bennett was my mentor and greatly influenced my thinking and living. Writing in the 60s, as a polymath he was able to comment insightfully on the human situation from a developmental perspective.
Other relevant titles: *The Sevenfold Work, Enneagram Studies, Witness*

Berne, Eric, *Games People Play*, Penguin, 1964.
Insights into human behaviour – we are more devious than we believe!

Blake, Anthony, *The intelligent Enneagram*, Shambala, 1996.
My colleague and collaborator was Bennett's editor and co-author which positions him ideally to share insights into the structure and meaning of the enneagram.

Blake, Anthony and Varney John, *A Guide to Meaning Making*, Chris Kington, 2005.
Guide to LogoVisual Thinking in relation to education.
Other relevant title: *A Guide to Making Sense.*

Bohm, David, *On Dialogue*, Routledge, 1996.
A respected scientist, he discovered something about the limits of ordinary discussion and the value of exploratory dialogue, of which he was a pioneer.

Bohm, David, *Wholeness and the Implicate Order*, Routledge and Kegan Paul, 1980.
A valuable perspective on the nature of wholeness and an impressive view of order in the physical world.

Bortoff, Henri, *Wholeness and Nature*, Floris, 1996.
Thought provoking book that carefully reveals the difference of perception that can come about when we think in terms of wholeness.

Campbell, Joseph, *Hero with a Thousand Faces*, The World Library, 2008.
A powerful review of universal myth and legend that postulates a singular 'monomyth' that is shared with cultures around the world. The hero's journey as the basis of story and purpose, pointing to the meaning of life.

Capra, Fritjof, *The Systems View of Life*, Cambridge University Press, 2014.
Capra brings accessible clarity to a scientist's sophisticated understanding of the joined-up nature of living systems in which we are embedded.
Other useful titles: *Tao of Physics, The Web of Life*.

Carse, James, *Finite and Infinite Games*, Free Press, 1986.
An alternative way of distinguishing different paradigms.

Castenada, Carlos, *Journey to Ixtlan*, Penguin, 1974.
Cult books from the 80s tell the story of the author's studies of Don Juan's shamanic teaching – deep insights from an alternative reality! Full of little gems.
And 10 other titles

Carter, Martin; Munday, Mayblin, *Systems, Management and Change*, Harper and Row, 1984.
A useful Open University primer on systems thinking.

Collins, Jim, *Good to Great*, Random House, 2001.
Well researched perspective on what influences produce consistently outstanding results in major organisations – gives point to philosophical/psychological considerations.

Csikszentmihalyi, Mihaly, *Flow*, Harper and Row, 1990.
Explores the concept of flow as a state of being to which to aspire: a quality that underpins extraordinary human achievement.

De Bono, Edward, *Lateral Thinking* (& many other of his titles), Penguin, 1970.
A prolific author and contributor to creative thinking. Originator of the term Lateral Thinking, which widely influenced education and management at the end of the 20th century.

De Geus, Ari, *The Living Company*, Harvard Business School Press, 2002.
The idea that organisation is a life-form that needs to be nurtured (illustrated by research that highlights the brevity of life of most organisations).

Douglas, Mary, *Thinking in Circles*, Yale University Press, 2007.
Looks at the cyclic nature of traditional story-telling that is relevant to the Ring-Composition of LogoVisual Thinking (LVT).

Drath, Wilfred, *The Deep Blue Sea: Rethinking the Source of Leadership*, Jossey-Bass 2001
Clear and startling view of how leadership has evolved and where we need to find it in these times of great change

Frankl, Viktor, *Man's Search for Meaning*, Rider, 2004.
In this amazing testimony to humanity's resilience, Frankl reveals something of its source and potential.

Fritz, Robert, *Path of Least Resistance*, Stillpoint, 1987.
Meeting Fritz was illuminating for me, as was this simple explanation of a principle of effective action.

Fromm, Erich, *The Art of Loving*, Unwin, 1976.
Insightful philosophy on basic human attitudes and behaviour, all clearly explained. Other useful title: *The Fear of Freedom*.

Galway, Timothy, *Inner Game of Work*, Texere, 2002.
Practical philosophy of action brought up to date and into context in readily graspable form.

Gilligan, Stephen and Dilts Robert, *The Hero's Journey*, Crown House, 2010.
An excellent 'course' in thinking about your hero's journey and a fair complement to my present book. This is a useful counterpoint – a different perspective that will enrich your understanding.

Harari, Yuval Noah, *Sapiens*, Vintage, 2015.
Broad history of humanity gives an 'Off-world' and out of time perspective of our current civilisation and where we may be headed. Sits alongside Lent's 'Patterning Instinct'.

Henry, Jane (editor), *Creative Management*, Sage, 1993.
Useful collection of chapters from noteworthy authors of late C20th gives a valuable overview of avant guard management thinking.

Heidegger, Martin, *What is called Thinking*, Harper Row, 1968.
Useful as a reference to one of the great philosophers of the 20th century.

Hide, Lewis, *The Gift*, Vintage, 1983.
An alternative view that vividly illustrates how, by commoditising property, we deprive ourselves of the life-enhancing gift of creativity.

Johnson, Thomas H./Broms Anders, *Profit Beyond Measure*, Nicolas Brealey, 2000.
Insights into the wholeness of the Toyota Production system that was once the envy of all manufacturers.

Knowles, Richard N., *The Leadership Dance*, Centre for Self-Organising Leadership, 2002.
A clear case study of how change of thinking brings changed behaviour, liberating people to achieve much more than control and command structures allow. (Systematic application of methods developed from Krone based on Bennett).

Kuchinski, Saul, *Systematics*, Claymont Communications, 1987.
Looks at a specific aspect of Bennett's work applied to the world of organisations. In some ways foreshadowed what Dick Knowles was able to enact.

Laloux, Frederic, *Reinventing Organisations*, Nelson Parker, 2014.
A powerful dissertation on how historical forms of organisation have evolved which suggests we are at the threshold of an evolutionary step – which the book goes on to describe.

Lent, Jeremy, *The Patterning Instinct*, Prometheus, 2017.
Broad perspective of cultural history and where we are today, Lent's off-world view illuminates something of our current crisis. Sits alongside Harari's 'Sapiens'.

Levi, Primo, *If this is a Man*, Abacus, 1987.
Acutely observed details of humanity in extremis (in Auschwitz) give valuable insights into our human condition, masterfully expressed and examined.

Low, Albert, *Zen and Creative Management*, Charles E Tuttle, 1976.
Low (as well as Kuchinski and Knowles) provide successive interpretations of the application of Bennett's systematics (and other ideas) to the world of work as they address the issues in which their authors were engaged.

Maturana, Humberto R. and Varela Francisco J., *The Tree of Knowledge*, Shambhala, 1998.
An extraordinary and influential book that summarises cognition from a biological perspective in a way that projects onto the evolutionary trends of living systems, revealing the concept that we create the world we occupy.

Meadows, Donella, *Thinking in Systems*, Earthscan, 2009.
Wonderful introduction to and overview of systems thinking from one of its great champions, not merely as a way of understanding complex wholes but of relating with them practically.

Owen, Harrison, *Open Space Technology*, Berrett Koehler, 1997.
A very effective way of engaging people in collaborative enquiry that opens up possibilities to embrace diversity to co-create shared solutions.

Persig, Robert, *Zen and the Art of Motorcycle Maintenance*, Corgi, 1976.
Published in 1974 this reflection on life and meaning was hugely influential and continues to inspire today.

Roam, Dan, *Back of the Napkin*, Marchall Cavendish, 2009.
Very useful and comprehensive review of visual thinking techniques.

Salamatov, Yuri, *TRIZ The Right Solution At The Right Time*, Insytec, 1999.
TRIZ is commonly misrepresented and misinterpreted but this book is close to the source. Somewhat quaint English does not obscure the profound methodology.

Shah, Idries, *Pleasantries of Mulla Nasrudin*, Pan Picador, 1975.
Spirituality without religion - A collection of titles that are valuable through coming from a different tradition than the bulk of western thought, providing extraordinary stimulus to think afresh.
Also by Shah, *Tales of the Dervishes,* Jonathan Cape, 1968 and many other titles

Sibbet, David, *Visual Meetings*, John Wiley and Sons, 2010.
Comprehensive introduction to use of visual representation of ideas, particularly as used to facilitate communications in meetings.

Stacey, Ralph, *Complexity and Creativity in Organizations*, Berrett Koehler, 1996.
Scientifically sound analysis of the way organisations work, in systemic terms.

Tate, William, *The Search for Leadership*, Triarchy Press, 2009.
Challenges the commonly held view that leadership is linked to power and suggests that it is a systemic quality.

Vail, Peter, *Managing as a Performing Art*, Jossey-Bass, 2009.
The idea of art and performance being what management is about run rather counter to conventional wisdom and thus provides a challenge to our worldview.

Wheatley, Margaret, *Leadership and the New Science*, Berrett Koehler, 1992.
Scientist and systems thinker with a valuable perspective on organisational learning and leadership. Wheatley makes the science readily understandable and maps it onto the way we organise, giving the possibility of a new paradigm.

Weisbord, Marvin R. & Janoff Sandra, *Future Search*, Berrett Koehler, 1995.
A very useful guide to running collaborative design events for organisations or communities, engaging people in shaping their futures. How to get conversations going that explore issues.

Index

Note: Locators in *italics* represent diagrams in the text.